DOING
CANADA
PROUD

DOING
CANADA
PROUD

The Second Boer War and the
Battle of Paardeberg

COLONEL BERND HORN

— CANADIANS AT WAR —

DUNDURN
TORONTO

Editor: Cheryl Hawley
Design: Jesse Hooper
Printer: Webcom

Library and Archives Canada Cataloguing in Publication

Horn, Bernd, 1959-
    Doing Canada proud : the Second Boer War and the Battle of Paardeberg / by Bernd Horn.

(Canadians at war)
Includes bibliographical references and index.
Issued also in electronic formats.
ISBN 978-1-4597-0577-7

    1. South African War, 1899-1902--Juvenile literature. 2. South African War, 1899-1902--Participation, Canadian--Juvenile literature. 3. Canada. Canadian Army. Royal Canadian Regiment--Juvenile literature. 4. Paardeberg, Battle of, South Africa, 1900--Participation, Canadian--Juvenile literature. 5. South African War, 1899-1902--Regimental histories—Canada--Juvenile literature. I. Title. II. Series: Canadians at war (Toronto, Ont.)

DT1908.P33H67 2012   j968.04'84   C2012-904595-0

1   2   3   4   5   16   15   14   13   12

Conseil des Arts du Canada   Canada Council for the Arts

Canada

ONTARIO ARTS COUNCIL
CONSEIL DES ARTS DE L'ONTARIO

We acknowledge the support of the **Canada Council for the Arts** and the **Ontario Arts Council** for our publishing program. We also acknowledge the financial support of the **Government of Canada** through the **Canada Book Fund** and **Livres Canada Books**, and the **Government of Ontario** through the **Ontario Book Publishing Tax Credit** and the **Ontario Media Development Corporation**.

Care has been taken to trace the ownership of copyright material used in this book. The author and the publisher welcome any information enabling them to rectify any references or credits in subsequent editions.

J. Kirk Howard, President

Printed and bound in Canada.

VISIT US AT
Dundurn.com | *Definingcanada.ca* | *@dundurnpress* | *Facebook.com/dundurnpress*

Dundurn	Gazelle Book Services Limited	Dundurn
3 Church Street, Suite 500	White Cross Mills	2250 Military Road
Toronto, Ontario, Canada	High Town, Lancaster, England	Tonawanda, NY
M5E 1M2	L41 4XS	U.S.A. 14150

CONTENTS

ACKNOWLEDGEMENTS

ONCE AGAIN I MUST TAKE SOME TIME UP FRONT TO THANK THOSE WHO have provided assistance behind the scenes in a number of ways. Any project of this nature is never a solitary endeavour. I wish to acknowledge those who have provided their time, expertise, guidance, and assistance in helping me finish this book.

I would like to thank Chris Johnson for his detailed map work. He has retired from the "business" and I will miss his skilled hand. I would also be remiss if I did not thank Dr. Emily Spencer for her help with research, as well as her excellent advice and feedback on the manuscript. I also need to thank Major Jim McInnis and museum curator Claus Breede, from The RCR Regimental Headquarters and The RCR Museum respectively, for their assistance in providing access to documents and photographs.

I must also highlight the incredible work of the Dundurn editorial and design team, specifically the editorial director, Michael Carroll, and copy editor, Cheryl Hawley, who turned a raw manuscript into the polished product that you hold in your hands.

Finally, as always, I wish to thank Kim for her continuing tolerance and patience of my never-ending projects and historical pursuits.

INTRODUCTION

THE BULLETS ZINGED PAST JEFF FULLER, FORCING HIM TO PUSH HIS body closer to the hard-packed dirt. Some of the bullets zipped by his head, while others chewed up the dirt beside him or ate away at the small termite mound he was hiding behind. As he tried to make himself small and insignificant, on what now seemed to be a very open and exposed South African veldt, Fuller actually tried to will himself deeper into the ground. He attempted to mould his body to every dent, depression, and crack.

He felt completely helpless. Every time he so much as lifted his head, even an inch, so that he could peek around the reddish-brown termite mound to try and see who was firing at him, he would attract the attention of what seemed to be every Boer rifleman dug-in at Paardeberg Drift. Fuller finally gave up even trying to raise his rifle to fire back. As long as he remained still the bullets that whizzed by him like angry hornets left him alone.

As Fuller lay on the hot earth he looked sideways. He could see several other British and Canadian soldiers, dressed in khaki, lying

Library and Archives Canada (LAC), PA 181414.

An RCR soldier returning enemy fire.

IMPORTANT FACTS

Veldt

The term veldt originates from the Afrikaans (originally Dutch) word *veld*, which has a literal translation meaning "field." Veldt refers to the wild, wide-open areas of South Africa and southern Africa that are covered with natural vegetation, such as grass and low scrub. The term veldt is similar to terms like the Canadian Prairie or the Australian Outback.

on the ground tying to avoid the attention of the Boer marksman. Some stirred but others lay completely still. They were not as fortunate as Fuller and had been killed in the foolish advance against the strong Boer defensive position.

The intensity of the early morning sun was already beginning to have an effect on Fuller. Despite the situation he found himself in, or perhaps because of it, he suddenly forgot his dangerous predicament and remembered how hungry he was. This realization consumed him with anger. They had marched all through the night — ceaselessly crunching across the endless veldt. Time had just dragged on. The sand in his socks chaffed his feet, which seemed like they were on fire the whole time. He thought his thirst would drive him crazy, and at the sporadic halts there was no water wagon or anywhere to refill his canteen.

Then, just when he thought he could go no further, as dawn began to peak over the horizon, they halted. Fuller had just taken off his worn boots, socks, and puttees to air out his battered feet and was looking forward to something to eat when the alarm was sounded. The enemy — the Boers, who they had been chasing for days — were trapped at Paardeberg Drift. Everyone scrambled to put on their boots and rush to the front line.

Fuller and his comrades had crossed the Modder River. Despite its muddy, lazy appearance the current was actually quite fast. Fuller had struggled to cross. He pulled himself along the rope that had been installed, the current pulling at his clothes making footing difficult. As he struggled up the opposite bank, tired and wet with his khaki uniform clinging to him making movement cumbersome, he momentarily forgot his fatigue and hunger and got caught up in the excitement of the attack. He joined a group of Canadians rushing forward to where some British troops had already taken cover.

Up until that moment the war hadn't been real. When he had joined up in Toronto, what seemed like ages ago, it was all excitement and adventure. He thought of the prospect of going to an exotic land and fighting with the famed British regulars. All of his friends and colleagues had congratulated him on his decision to serve queen and country, and they wished him well. Many of his friends actually told him how they envied his opportunity.

Fuller imagined how the campaign would be. He thought of daring deeds, heroic actions, and adventure. That idea died quickly enough. The voyage from Canada to South Africa had been a huge disappointment. The ship was unfit for cattle, much less humans. It was small, squalid, and bobbed like a cork in the water. The constant sound and smell of individuals being seasick made a bad situation worse. And just when it seemed things were as bad as they could get, the commanding officer had made them walk around in bare feet to toughen their soles — but all they achieved was really bad sunburns.

Upon arrival in South Africa, Fuller's concept of adventure deteriorated further. The reality of soldiering began to sink in. Their days were filled with monotony and boredom. Endless guard duty and

FROM THE INTELLIGENCE FILES

Boers

In 1652 Jan van Riebeeck, an agent for the Dutch East India Company, established a trading station on the Cape of Good Hope, at the tip of South Africa. By 1707 Cape Colony had a population of 1,779. The Dutch colony was so prosperous that the agricultural market became saturated, and slave labour left little opportunity for employment as manual labour. Many of the white farmers were forced to become *trekboeren*, wandering farmers who migrated out to the high veldt to find opportunities that did not exist in Cape Colony.

The Boers who migrated had a difficult life. They constantly fought with the indigenous African people. They were also hostile toward the government, which attempted to control their movements and economic prosperity. Their cultural separation from the population of Cape Colony widened until, by the end of the 18th century, both groups were dramatically different. However, both continued to use Afrikaans (a mixture of Dutch, other languages, and indigenous African) as their official language.

In 1806 Cape Colony became a British possession. The Boers quickly became disgruntled with British policies and rule, particularly when slavery was abolished. Between 1835 and 1843 approximately 12,000 Boers left Cape Colony for the veldt, a migration commonly called the Great Trek. The Boers eventually established new settlements and their own republics. In 1852 the British government recognized the independence of the settlers in the Transvaal (later called the South African Republic). Two years later, in 1854, the British also recognized the independence of the Boers who had settled in the proximity of the Vaal and Orange rivers (an area later designated as the Orange Free State).

Today, descendants of the Boers are commonly referred to as Afrikaners.

camp chores ate up most of their time. The heat, lack of water, and overabundance of insects made their daily life miserable. The fine African sand worked its way into everything and there was nothing one could do to keep their bodies or equipment clean. To add to the misery, small dust devils, like miniature tornados, would spool up and engulf everything in their path in a dense cloud of dirt.

Fuller actually laughed to himself. How they had all longed for action! Boy did they want a chance to fight it out with the Boers. If only they could see some combat. And then the war got real. As he rushed forward with his comrades, the air was suddenly filled with the ugly zip and zing of unseen hornets. It took Fuller a few minutes to realize they were bullets actually looking for him. But the sudden thud of a bullet hitting the soldier to his right brought the realization of his mortality home. Fuller took a few more steps and then dove behind the termite mound.

As he lay there, pondering his adventure, he found himself drifting off to sleep in the intense heat. He woke with a start as thunder boomed overhead and he was suddenly drenched by a terrific downpour. Could he get any more miserable? Fuller

The RCR Museum and Archives.

wondered once again how he had gotten himself into this predicament. Despite his surroundings he couldn't help smiling ... "For queen and country," he said aloud to no one other than himself.

Suddenly he heard shouts. It seemed like there would finally be some action. Fuller tensed. A charge — they were going to charge the enemy! *Okay*, he said to himself, *let's see how this works out*. As he prepared to lift himself off the ground his nerves began to shake. "You can do this," he muttered. But then he couldn't help but ask, "How did I get myself into this mess?"

Boer riflemen engage British and Canadian troops.

IMPORTANT FACTS

South Africa

South Africa is the southern tip of the African continent. It is a constitutional democracy, comprised of nine provinces. Its coastline is approximately 2,800 kilometres long and borders both the Atlantic and Indian Oceans. South Africa is a diverse country that has 11 official languages. Although English is commonly used, particularly for business, it is only the fifth-most-spoken South African language.

Bartolomeu Dias, a Portuguese explorer, discovered the southernmost tip of Africa in May 1488 and named it Cape of Storms. The Portuguese king renamed it Cape of Good Hope, since it was the route that led from Europe to the riches of the East Indies and Orient.

South Africa was colonized in 1652, when Jan van Riebeeck established a Dutch East India Company supply station and trading post at the Cape of Good Hope, which became Cape Town.

The British seized the colony in 1795 during the Napoleonic Wars, because of its strategic value as a port and naval station on the way to its possessions in Australia and India. Britain returned Cape Town to the Dutch in 1803, but annexed the colony three years later in 1806. The British encouraged settlement and continued to push the borders of its new colony, creating continual conflict with the indigenous tribes.

With the discovery of diamonds in 1867 and gold in 1884, the tensions between Britain and the Boer Republics intensified, leading to the First and Second Boer Wars.

In 1909 the British Parliament passed the South Africa Act, creating the Union of South Africa (encompassing Cape Colony and Natal, as well as the republics of Orange Free State and the Transvaal), a dominion of the British Empire. The Statute of Westminster, passed in 1931, granted South Africa independence from Britain.

In 1948 the National Party was elected to power. It strengthened the racial segregation that had begun under Dutch and British colonial rule. The government established three racial classifications of people (white, coloured [people of Asian or mixed racial ancestry], and black) with rights and limitations for each. A white minority controlled a black majority. The rigid system of segregation, called apartheid, ensured the white and coloured population of South Africa enjoyed greater rights, freedoms, and economic prosperity than the African descendants who represented almost 80 percent of the population. Apartheid was strictly enforced, despite widespread criticism.

South Africa became a republic (no longer a member of the British Commonwealth) on May 31, 1961, following a referendum in which only whites participated. The country's apartheid policy became increasingly controversial and South Africa became the target of international boycotts, both economic and political. Government oppression of blacks also created an opposition that resulted in a bloody long-standing conflict.

The National Party government finally took the first step toward ending apartheid in 1990. It lifted the ban on the African National Congress (ANC) and other political organizations that represented the political opposition to the government, and released Nelson Mandela, the leader of the ANC, from prison after 27 years of incarceration for sabotage. Negotiations followed and the government eventually repealed its apartheid legislation. South Africa held its first open election in 1994, which the ANC won with an overwhelming majority. The ANC has remained in power ever since and South Africa has rejoined the British Commonwealth.

CHAPTER 1

Going to War

ON OCTOBER 11, 1899, BRITAIN OFFICIALLY WENT TO WAR WITH THE republics of Transvaal and the Orange Free State. Conflict in South Africa had been brewing for a long time, and by the summer of 1899 the relationship between the British and the Boers had deteriorated dramatically, partially over the denial of civic and social rights of the Uitlanders (non-residents) who were mainly British citizens living and/or working in the Boer republics. This insult to the fair treatment and democratic freedom of British subjects was too much for the government of England to bear. The fact that large deposits of precious minerals had recently been discovered in the breakaway territories did not help ease the tension.

The British were not worried about going to war. Their political and military leadership were confident that the conflict would end quickly. In the opinion of British military commanders, the Boers were just farmers. Lord Dundonald, the leader of the British forces, doubted the capability of his opponents so much that he actually asked an officer of the locally raised scouts if "the Boers would fight when they saw her majesty's troops."

IMPORTANT FACTS

Transvaal

The Transvaal Republic was the informal name given to the independent Boer state. Starting in the 1830s, Boers who wanted to escape what they felt were harsh British rules, regulations, and governance fled from Cape Colony to the open veldt, where they were beyond British control and could form their own small Boer republics. Their settlement of the veldt led to confrontation with the indigenous tribes, but the Boers' superior military arms and technology allowed them to quickly defeat the indigenous population. The British recognized the Boers' independence in 1852, with the passing of the Sand River Convention.

When gold was discovered at Tati, in April 1868, the government of Transvaal extended their territory so that they could fully control the goldfield. In 1877 the British annexed the Transvaal, leading to the First Anglo-Boer War. The Boers won the conflict and, in accordance with the Pretoria Convention of 1881, regained their self-rule. Britain recognized their independence in 1884 as a result of the London Convention. However, renewed conflict in 1899 led to the Second Anglo-Boer War, which the Boers lost. As a result, the territory was once again annexed by the British on May 31, 1902. Eight years later, it became the Transvaal Province within the Union of South Africa.

The British arrogance quickly disappeared. The conflict did not go as they expected. In the autumn of 1899, British soldiers and politicians alike were shocked at the fighting ability of the Boers, who inflicted several humiliating and expensive defeats on the British Field Force. These unexpected "drubbings" pointed out that the British Army was unprepared to meet the challenges of modern warfare. The humiliating climax came during the week of December 10–15, 1899, when three separate British formations were decisively beaten at Stormberg, Magersfontein, and Colenso. These fateful seven days were appropriately called "Black Week."

The impact in South Africa was enormous. During Black Week the high commissioner in Capetown, Alfred, Lord Milner, sent an anxious telegraph cable to Joseph Chamberlain, the colonial secretary in London. "This is the worst blow we have sustained yet during the war," he wrote. Adding, "The impression it has created here is simply deplorable, and this is sure to be the case throughout the Colony." Milner's entry in his diary the next day had more than a hint of panic:

> December 12th [1899] — The news to-day is again extremely bad. There can be no doubt that General Gatacre's defeat on Sunday was a very severe one, and

the effect of a large number of British prisoners being taken through a rebel district of the Colony into the Orange Free State cannot but be most injurious. One consequence is that, as reported by various magistrates, armed men are leaving their homes in various parts of the eastern districts, and going to join the enemy.

Two days later he acknowledged that there was a "deep depression in loyal circles in consequence of the three disasters of the past week.... General Buller's defeat on the Tugela [River], coming on the top of Stormberg and Magersfontein, has been rather too much for the bravest." By Christmas he told Chamberlain, "The effects of the reverses at Stormberg, Magersfontein and Colenso is cumulative.... Even in the remotest country districts it is now known that

LAC, PA 128778.

At the Battle of Colenos, during "Black Week," the British artillery were caught in a deadly ambush that killed most of their horses and men.

IMPORTANT FACTS

Orange Free State

The Orange Free State was an independent Boer republic in southern Africa. Starting in the 1820s a large number of Boers left Cape Colony in search of grazing land, as well as to escape government control. About a decade later they were joined by more Boers, who fled Cape Colony during the Great Trek to escape British governance and restrictions.

The Boers reached an agreement with the local tribes to settle the land between the Vet and Vaal rivers. Despite the agreements, tensions arose between the Boers and indigenous tribes, which led to conflict. The Boers also had issues with the British government over sovereignty, boundaries, and governance of the indigenous tribes. Nonetheless, in 1848 Britain proclaimed that the region between the Orange and Vaal rivers would be recognized as the Orange River Sovereignty. More importantly, on February 17, 1854, following the granting of independence of the Transvaal Republic, the British also declared that the Orange River Sovereignty was officially independent. Six days later, after the signing of the Orange River Convention, it became formally known as the Orange Free State. Bloemfontein was its capital.

Despite their economic and political success, or perhaps because of it, the Boers remained in conflict with the British. The British annexed the Orange Free State in 1902, at the end of the Second Anglo-Boer War. On May 31, 1902, with the signing of the Treaty of Vereeniging, the Orange Free State ceased to exist as an independent entity.

the enemy have had great successes." He ominously added, "The spirit of rebellion has received an enormous impetus — even in districts hitherto comparatively quiet."

The effect elsewhere in the empire was similarly dramatic. "The military situation is without doubt at this moment most grave and critical," reported Winston Churchill, the future prime minister of Britain, who was a war correspondent at the beginning of the conflict. "We have been at war three weeks, [and] the army that was to have defended Natal, and was indeed expected to repulse the invaders with terrible loss, is blockaded and bombarded in its fortified camp." He added, "At nearly every point along the circle of the frontiers the Boers have advanced and the British retreated. Wherever we have stood we have been surrounded.... All this is mainly the result of being unready.... It is also due to an extraordinary under-estimation of the strength of the Boers." England turned to their former colonies in a desperate plea for troops — no longer for political purposes, but for fighting men.

Despite the British military problems in South Africa, patriotic fervour ran high in Canada. However, not all Canadians wanted to join the latest imperial adventure. For Prime Minister Wilfrid Laurier the entire issue of supporting the latest British war effort was problematic. He realized that supporting an overseas military venture was costly — in money, blood, and national unity. There were large segments of Canadian society that were opposed to providing military forces to support the empire, many of them francophones in Quebec.

Despite his efforts, Laurier could not keep the country out of the war. English Canada insisted that Canada support Britain. This swell of imperial zeal was fuelled by the scheming of the British general officer commanding (GOC) military forces in Canada, Major-General Hutton, and the governor general, the Earl of Minto. Hutton went so far as to write to the British colonial secretary, "Having perhaps better cause to know this intense feeling of military enthusiasm and deep rooted loyalty than most Canadians I especially warned the Minister of Militia and several others of the Cabinet of the consequences of any hesitation upon their part to offer troops."

FROM THE INTELLIGENCE FILES

Wilfrid Laurier

Sir Wilfrid Laurier was Canada's seventh prime minister. He had the distinction of being the nation's first francophone prime minister. Born on November 20, 1841, he was chosen as the leader of the Liberal Party in 1887. Through his strong personal following in Quebec and elsewhere in Canada he was able to build up the party, which he led to victory in the 1896 election.

Known as a political moderate, Laurier followed a path of conciliation and compromise between English and French Canada. His vision for the country revolved around individual liberty and a decentralized federalism. He also worked hard to ensure that Canada was an autonomous country within the British Empire

Laurier remained in power until the Liberal Party defeat in 1911, becoming the fourth-longest-serving prime minister of Canada. However, with four federal election victories, he won more consecutive federal elections than any other prime minister. His 15 years as prime minister remains the longest unbroken term of office for a Canadian prime minister. Furthermore, his almost 45 years of service as a minister of Parliament (1874–1919) remains a record for the House of Commons. Laurier was also the longest-serving leader of a major federal political party (almost 32 years). Not surprisingly, his portrait adorns the Canadian five dollar bill. Wilfrid Laurier died of a stroke on February 17, 1919.

When war was declared on October 11, 1899, Laurier had little choice, unless he wished to destroy any chance of a Liberal re-election, to commit Canadian forces to the war effort. As a result, after two days of heated Cabinet discussion, on October 14 the government announced that it would send a Canadian military contingent to South Africa. The details, however, still had to be worked out.

Battles of the 19th Century, 1902.

Although the Boers lacked the appearance of professional soldiers, they were all excellent horsemen and crack shots with a rifle. They proved to be a difficult foe.

Joseph Chamberlain, the British colonial secretary, immediately accepted the Canadian offer to dispatch troops to South Africa. He cabled the governor general of Canada and explained that the contribution should consist of infantry soldiers. Moreover, he directed that the Canadian contingent be organized into units of approximately 125 men, with one captain and no more than three subalterns for each respective unit. He also insisted that the whole force could be commanded by an officer of the rank no higher than major. Chamberlain dictated that the cost of mounting and equipping, as well as transport to South Africa, was to be paid for by Canada. However, once the troops disembarked they would become imperial troops and provided pay, rations, clothing, supplies, and ammunition by the British government.

Quite simply, the Canadian contingent, like all colonial contingents, was to be absorbed into British units and formations. This meant that Canadian and other colonial troops would be used largely for garrison, picket, and rear-area security tasks, since British regulars had little faith in the military capability of militiamen and even less in colonials. The British government wanted colonial contingents for political reasons, for a show of imperial unity not for their military application or worth. "We do not want the men," wrote Chamberlain to the Canadian governor general, "the whole point of the offer would be lost unless it was endorsed by the Government of the Colony."

The British direction was ignored. Canadians had developed a national identity and they pushed for a strong unified Canadian contingent. Surprisingly, it was Governor General Minto who pressed the Canadian prime minister to acknowledge popular opinion and insist that Britain accept a Canadian contribution worthy of Canada's position in the empire. "You will see from the cable that it is evidently intended that the Canadian troops on arriving in South Africa should be attached to the different units which they represent, and that they should not remain constituted as a Canadian contingent," advised

FROM THE INTELLIGENCE FILES

Anti-War Movement

Although many Canadians were enthusiastic about joining the Imperial adventure, and pushed the government to join England's fight in South Africa, many others were opposed to the war. The most vocal group was the French Canadians. Their chief spokesman was Henri Bourassa, a well-educated and articulate young Liberal minister of Parliament, who was Prime Minister Laurier's protege in Quebec. As the efforts to involve Canada in the Boer War increased, Bourassa grew very vocal in his attack on the pro-war stand and the "Imperialists."

The French Canadians were sensitive to the underlying implications of the war, and identified with the Boers' cause of protecting themselves and their culture from the aggressive British. They also did not see any why Canada should take an interest in far away Transvaal or the Orange Free State. It was hard for the French Canadians to understand how one could be loyal to the British Empire and Canada at the same time. Moreover, participation in a war could also lead to the hated and feared conscription, which would force French Canadians to fight overseas for a cause they did not believe in.

French Canadians were not the only voices of opposition. Many English Canadians did not want to have anything to do with South Africa either. Why should young Canadians die and taxpayers bear the burden for something that had nothing to do with them? Others felt that it would be too disruptive to agriculture and emerging industry, both of which were just recovering from a 20-year depression. Finally, there were the pacifists, like the Doukhobor and Mennonite communities, who opposed all war.

FROM THE INTELLIGENCE FILES

Imperial Interference?

Prime Minister Laurier was cautious and slow to react to the British request for Canadian participation in the war in South Africa. He knew that entering the war would create friction with French Canadians and the anti-war element in Canada. He was also aware that he must do something. However, his ability to control events was lessened when the general officer commanding (GOC) the Canadian Militia, who was a British officer, began a secret campaign to pull Canada into the war.

Behind the scenes, GOC General E.T.H. Hutton had secretly been drafting a plan to send a large Canadian contingent to South Africa. At every military mess dinner and inspection that he attended, Hutton discussed the possibility of sending Canadian troops. Hutton was also quietly working up hopes by letting the militia know that he had a well-organized plan for an expeditionary force and that supportive certain individuals were to be in it.

On October 3, 1899, the *Canadian Military Gazette* (the widely distributed newspaper of the Canadian Militia) published details of Hutton's secret plan, adding confidently that the government was likely to send the force. At the same time, by a convenient "coincidence," a Colonial Office memo arrived in Canada, thanking the Dominion for offering troops – which of course it had not done. But this memo somehow found its way into the public domain. Evidence pointed to Hutton's behind-the-scenes manipulations, which was a clear challenge to the authority of the Canadian government. Once the Canadian government had enough evidence, Prime Minister Laurier insisted that the British recall their meddling GOC.

Unfortunately, the damage was already done. Political pressure mounted. When war between Britain and the Boers broke out in early October, and Canada had not yet done anything, another frenzy of pro-war agitation exploded. Laurier had little choice. After two stormy days of Cabinet meetings, on October 14 he finally announced that Canada would send an official contingent of 1,000 volunteers. Canada was at war.

Minto. "I think it would be better if troops are to be offered at all, that they should be offered as a Canadian contingent to act as such."

Laurier took the wise counsel and, on October 18, his Cabinet approved the establishment and deployment of a regiment of infantry, namely the 2nd (Special Service) Battalion, The Royal Canadian Regiment (RCR) — 1,000-strong commanded by Lieutenant-Colonel William D. Otter. It was to deploy as a distinct, integral Canadian unit. In fact, the 2nd Battalion, The RCR, consisted of only 100 permanent force members. The rest of the Battalion were volunteers.

Although largely a volunteer force, the Battalion was nonetheless established as a permanent force unit due to the overwhelming nationalist sentiment, as well as the overseas deployment and nature

FROM THE INTELLIGENCE FILES

The First Anglo-Boer War

The Anglo-Boer War, known by the Afrikaans as the "First Freedom War," took place from December 16, 1880, until March 23, 1881. In 1877, Britain annexed both the Transvaal and Orange Free State, spurred by large discoveries of gold and diamond deposits and the race against other European powers for colonies in Africa.

Facing hostile local tribes who were waiting for an opportunity to rise up in rebellion and the British, the Boers feared a two-front war they could not win. The British defeat of the Zulu nation in July 1879 provided the Boers with the opportunity they needed. On December 16, 1880, the Boers revolted and declared their independence from the United Kingdom. Within days the Boers attacked a British convoy, and between January 22, 1880, and January 6, 1881, British Army garrisons throughout the Transvaal were besieged.

There were only three main engagements in the short war. The first was the Battle of Laing's Nek on January 28, 1881, and the second at Ingogo River on February 8, 1881. On February 14, the Boers called a truce to pursue peace negotiations. Although the British government was conciliatory and offered terms, the local British commander decided to use the pause while waiting for the Boer response to attack them and give the British government a position of power in the negotiations. However, the final battle at Majuba Hill, on February 27, 1881, was a disaster for the British.

After the British defeat at Majuba Hill, hostilities continued until March 6, 1881, when a truce was put in place, based on the terms of the February 14th truce. The British government decided that it was not interested in a distant war that would require reinforcements and money, and signed a peace treaty with the Boers on March 6, 1881. The British recognized Boer self-government and the Boers accepted British control over African affairs and native districts. The Pretoria Convention, ratified on October 25, 1881, resulted in the withdrawal of British troops.

of the mission. But in the end the government took this decision to underline the fact that the Canadian troops did not simply represent a levy of British Army recruits, but a distinct Canadian contingent.

Reluctantly, and with a great deal of Minto's prodding, the British government and the British War Office accepted the Canadian contribution. They also agreed to the official request to keep the Canadian contingent together as much as possible. However, the British commander-in-chief in South Africa cautioned that he could not "guarantee that the [Canadian] Contingent shall always be kept together during operations." He added, the "general must be free to dispose of the force to the best advantage." The Canadian government acknowledged and accepted the warning.

IMPORTANT FACTS

Colony

The word *colony* is derived from the Latin word *colōnia*, which comes from the word *colōnus*, meaning colonist but usually referring to a farmer. Colonies are actually territories that are under the political control of a state.

Territories that were discovered and were not under the control of an existing country were claimed, possessed, and governed by the state that "discovered" the territory. Colonies took on many forms, such as naval stations or military bases and trading outposts. They were often an important source of raw materials. But at the heart of the definition is the concept of creating settlements by sending people from the home country to the newly claimed territory.

IMPORTANT FACTS

British Empire

The British Empire was made up of all the colonies, dominions, protectorates, and territories that were administered, owned, and politically controlled by the United Kingdom. The empire was built from the overseas colonies and trading outposts that Britain established in the late 1500s and early 1600s. At the height of its power the British Empire was the largest empire in history, and it remained a world power for much of its existence. By 1922 it controlled a quarter of the world's population and comprised almost a quarter of the earth's total land mass. For this reason it was often said that the "sun never sets on the British Empire." Not surprisingly, the legacy of the British Empire in terms of its cultural, linguistic, and political footprint is significant.

With the end of the Second World War, fiscal pressures and an international effort to decolonize led to the United Kingdom granting independence to many of its remaining colonies and territories. Today, most former British possessions have joined the British Commonwealth of Nations, which is a free association of independent states.

CHAPTER 2

Slow Beginnings

THE FIRST TASK WAS CREATING THE BATTALION TO SEND TO SOUTH Africa. Although mostly a volunteer force, as already mentioned, the Battalion had a core of 100 Regular serving soldiers who would act as the leadership and training cadre. The actual mobilization of the 2nd Battalion was astonishingly fast. This was particularly surprising since the unit was made up of eight companies (Coy) that were drawn from across Canada:

> "**A**" Coy raised in British Columbia and Manitoba;
> "**B**" Coy raised in London;
> "**C**" Coy raised in Toronto;
> "**D**" Coy raised in Ottawa and Kingston;
> "**E**" Coy raised in Montreal;
> "**F**" Coy raised in Quebec;
> "**G**" Coy raised in New Brunswick and Prince Edward Island; and
> "**H**" Coy raised in Nova Scotia.

FROM THE INTELLIGENCE FILES

The RCR

The Royal Canadian Regiment (RCR) is Canada's oldest serving regular force regiment, formed on December 21, 1883, to instruct the Canadian Militia. The regiment's first task was participation in suppressing of the North-West Rebellion in 1885. During the short conflict The RCR soldiers fought battles at Fish Creek, Cut Knife Creek, and Batoche.

In 1898 The RCR returned to the North-West, this time to Dawson Creek. The gold rush had attracted thousands of prospectors and entrepreneurs, who flooded into the Yukon Territory to make their fortune, overtaxing the North-West Mounted Police. The government sent in soldiers to help maintain law and order. Once the gold rush died down so did the need for the Royals.

However, the Royals were not idle for long. The war in South Africa prompted Canada to deploy a contingent called the 2nd (Special Service) Battalion, Royal Canadian Regiment of Infantry. It served with distinction during a one-year tour of duty, earning a special parade at Windsor Castle for its part in the victory at the Battle of Paardeberg.

The RCR also served in the First and Second World Wars, participating in many actions and once again serving with distinction. Unfortunately, the postwar peace did not last long. In 1951 The RCR once again deployed overseas, this time in Korea, where they fought a number of key engagements, most notably the battle of Kowang San. For its part in the Korean War, The RCR was awarded the battle honour Korea 1951–53.

Throughout the Cold War (1948–89), as the North Atlantic Treaty Organization (NATO) faced down the Soviet Union and its Warsaw Pact allies, The RCR were active at the Canadian garrison in Germany.

At home, the Royals deployed to Ottawa and Montreal during the October Crisis in October 1970, when FLQ terrorists threatened to spread violence in Ottawa and Quebec to attain their political goals. In the spring to fall of 1990, The RCR assisted when violence erupted in Oka, Quebec. Throughout its history, The RCR also assisted fellow Canadians faced with natural disasters as well as man-made emergencies, such as searching for missing peopled and hunting for fugitives.

The RCR has also participated in many peacekeeping and peace-stabilization missions, including tours in Cyprus from 1964–90 and the former Republic of Yugoslavia from 1991–99. Royals deployed in Operation Desert Shield and Operation Desert Storm from 1990–91.

In the new millennium, overseas duty exploded. The RCR sent personnel to Eritrea and Haiti on peace support missions, and has had a heavy presence in Afghanistan since 2006.

Throughout its 128-year history, The RCR has maintained a proud tradition of courage, duty, and professionalism.

On October 23, 1899, the different companies were ordered to assemble in Quebec City. Four days later the Battalion was formally established. Incredibly, the entire unit, numbering 41 officers and 998 enlisted ranks (for a total of 1,039), was loaded onto the SS *Sardinian* on October 30. The entire force was recruited, equipped, and embarked for deployment to South Africa in less than two weeks.

The troop transport was very quickly dubbed the "Sardine." It was anything but adequate. The converted cattle ship, reported Lieutenant-Colonel Otter, "proved to be a very slow ship, and greatly lacking in room and accommodation for the numbers on board … sanitary arrangements were particularly bad, and so crowded was the ship that parades or drills were matters of extreme difficulty."

The troops were even more critical. Private Frederick Ramsay revealed, "We are packed like sardines in our bunks and hammocks." Arthur Bennett wrote in a letter, "This boat is the greatest old tub to roll that was every built, she rolls around like an intoxicated man if there is the slightest swell…. Some of the fellows had it [seasickness] pretty badly, and for the first day thought they would die, and the next more afraid than ever in case they wouldn't." At the time they had no idea that this was a sign of things to come.

LAC, C-7981.

Members of "D" Company on parade.

IMPORTANT FACTS

LAC, PA-212769.

The SS Sardinian, *dubbed the "Sardine" by the troops because of its inadequate size and facilities.*

SS *Sardinian*

The SS *Sardinian* was built in 1875, for the Allan Line Steamship Company, as a passenger cargo vessel. The Allan Line of steamers was well-known at the turn of the century. *Sardinian* was 400 feet long and 42.3 feet wide. She made her maiden voyage from Liverpool to Quebec City and Montreal.

In addition to transporting Canadian soldiers to South Africa in 1899, the *Sardinian* also holds a special place in Canadian history. In 1901 the steamer carried Guglielmo Marconi and his radio equipment to Newfoundland. There, Marconi climbed to the top of Signal Hill, at the entrance to St. John's harbour, and made the first transatlantic radio transmission to Europe.

The *Sardinian* was sold to the Canadian Pacific Steamship Company in 1915, resold to Astoreca Azqueta, in Spain, in 1920, which reduced her to a coal hauler, then resold again to Compania Carbonera in 1934, and final sold as scrap in 1938.

When they arrived in Cape Town it became clear to the Canadians that the war was not going well. They soon heard how the Boers had repeatedly beaten the British Field Force.

The inexperienced Canadian volunteers entered what appeared to be a desperate struggle against a wily and very capable enemy. Nonetheless, the "green" Canadian soldiers were eager to get in to the fight. The Battalion disembarked at Cape Town on November 30, but it was not allowed to linger long. The desperate situation in the field necessitated their presence at the front. They entrained the next day for Belmont. But contrary to their expectations and desires, they were not deployed to battle. Instead, they spent the next two hot and monotonous months securing the lines of communication. Their battles were more with boredom, hunger, and the harsh environment than with the Boers. These conditions very quickly created morale problems.

Outpost duty was both demanding and particularly tedious. "Our present duties has I think a depressing effect upon the men — these duties consist of outpost fatigues and working parties and are very heavy," Otter wrote in the unit report. Private Ramsay explained, "We sleep in our tents with most of our clothes on and our accoutrements at

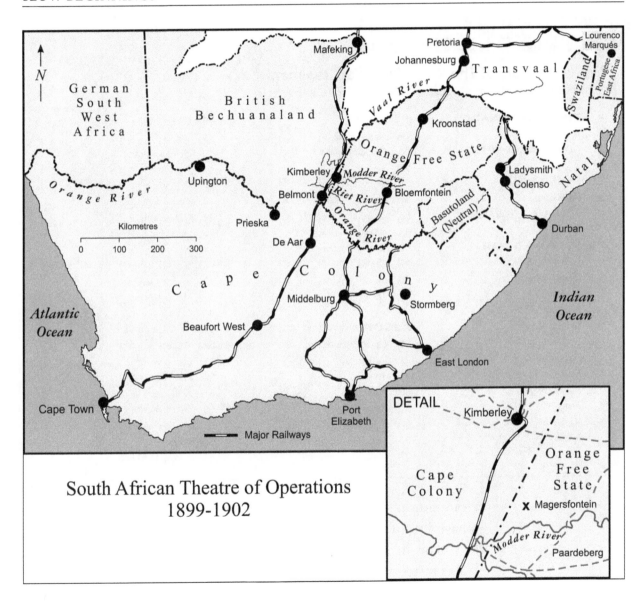

South African Theatre of Operations 1899-1902

Map by Chris Johnson.

FROM THE INTELLIGENCE FILES

Battle Honours of The Royal Canadian Regiment

(Italics indicates those Honours emblazoned on the Regimental Colours)

NORTHWEST CANADA

1. *Saskatchewan*
2. *North-West Canada, 1885*

SOUTH AFRICA

3. *Paardeberg*
4. *South Africa, 1899–1900*

FIRST WORLD WAR

5. *Ypres, 1915*
6. Gravenstafel
7. St. Julien
8. Festubert, 1915
9. *Mount Sorrel*
10. *Somme, 1916*
11. Pozieres
12. Flers-Courcelette
13. *Ancré Heights*
14. Arras, 1917
15. *Vimy, 1917*
16. Arieux
17. Scarpe, 1917

18. *Hill 70*
19. *Ypres, 1917*
20. *Passchendaele*
21. *Amiens*
22. Arras, 1918
23. Scarpe, 1918
24. Droucourt-Queant
25. *Hindenburg Line*
26. Canal du Nord
27. Cambrai, 1918
28. *Pursuit to Mons*
29. France and Flanders, 1915–18

SECOND WORLD WAR

30. *Landing in Sicily*
31. Valguarnera
32. Agira
33. Adrano
34. Regalbuto
35. Sicily, 1943
36. Landing at Reggio
37. *Motta Montecorvino*

38. Campobosso
39. Torella
40. *San Leonardo*
41. The Gully
42. Ortona
43. *Cassino II*
44. Gustav Line
45. Liri Valley
46. *Hitler Line*
47. *Gothic Line*
48. *Lamone Crossing*
49. Misano Ridge
50. *Rimini Line*
51. San Martino-San Lorenzo
52. Pisciatello
53. Fosso Vecchio
54. *Italy, 1943–45*
55. Apeldoorn
56. *North-West Europe, 1945*

KOREA

57. *Korea, 1951–53*

our side…. I haven't had my boots off for nearly two weeks and have forgotten what a bath is like."

The harsh environment and the inadequate logistical support also tested the troops. From the first day the Canadians faced conditions they would soon become only too familiar with. "Little or nothing to eat, stinking slushy water to drink, no tents for shelter on a hot summer day in Africa and a terrible rain storm," reported one participant. And when it was not raining there was the other constant irritant. "There is nothing but sand, sand, sand and a few little tufts of sage brush here and there and then there are sand storms," complained Private Jesse Briggs. "They are dense, choking, blinding and penetrate every crevice."

The South African environment was also very hard on the clothing. "The wear and tear upon clothing and boots is excessive and Canadian made clothing (khaki) is very much inferior to the English," stated a unit report. Both of these issues would become very problematic in short order.

The shortage of food was another major aggravation. "Things are going from bad to worse here in the way of grub," complained Private Bennett. "We are on poor rations and we are even on water rations." On a number of occasions Bennett passed on advice to those who may have been considering volunteering for the Second Contingent: "Well if the boys took my advice they would stay at home … for there is nothing here but a burning sun and desert storm…. This is the most forsaken country I have ever seen."

Lieutenant-Colonel Otter was another major aggravation. "How the boys dislike that man," revealed Private J.A. Perkins. Although experienced and a skilled trainer, he was dour and uninspiring. The men found him rigid and uncompromising. They chaffed at his discipline and endless drill. One letter home revealed a common complaint:

> The Colonel, who commands this regiment has lately taken it into his head that a march every day would do us some good and harden our feet, so at 4.30 p.m. every day we are paraded and marched off under the burning sun, over rocks and sand for about 10 miles, getting

back about 8 o'clock, which gives us exactly half an hour to get our supper and fix our blankets before the bugle sounds "lights-out." We are, of course, wet to the skin with perspiration and have no time to change, so sleep in our wet things, and as it gets cold as the deuce at night, the boys are all getting cold.

RCR troops doing rifle drill onboard the SS Sardinian, en route to South Africa.

Photographer James Cooper Mason, LAC, PA-173032.

Photographer S.M. Rogers, PA-185357.

*RCR camp at De Aar,
South Africa, 1900.*

They resented Otter's refusal to allow a dry canteen where additional food and drink could be purchased by the hungry troops — even though all other regimental camps had them. He would not even allow the YMCA to provide such a service. The men also felt he did not push his British superiors for better, more active employment. "I don't think much of Colonel Otter.... The boys call him the Old Woman and many other pretty stiff names," confided one soldier in a letter home. "He is too fond I think of giving the men too much marching, and that at a time when it interferes with a fellow's grub time."

FROM THE INTELLIGENCE FILES

LAC, C-20010.

Lieutenant-Colonel W.D. Otter, Commander First Canadian Contingent, the 2nd (Special Service) Battalion, The RCR.

General Sir William Dillon Otter

General Sir William Dillon Otter was born on December 3, 1843, near Corners, Upper Canada (present-day Ontario). He began his military career in the Toronto militia in 1864, when he joined the Queen's Own Rifles. In 1866, as the unit's adjutant, he saw his first action at the Battle of Ridgeway when the unit deployed against the invading Fenians. In 1883, when Canada established a small permanent force, Otter was appointed as the commander of the infantry school depot in Toronto. Two years later, Otter was sent to the North-West to serve in the North-West Rebellion.

Given command of a column to relieve the town of Battleford, Otter precipitated a battle at Cut Knife Creek, which he lost. His choice of ground, ineffective cannon, and a very mobile enemy who maximized the use of terrain caused him to suffer a humiliating defeat. This did not hurt his career. In 1893 he was appointed as the first commanding officer of The Royal Canadian Regiment of Infantry, and six years later, in 1899, the government selected Otter to lead the 2nd (Special Service) Battalion, The Royal Canadian Regiment (2 RCR) overseas during the second Anglo-Boer War. Although he was unpopular with his troops, Otter and 2 RCR were highly regarded by their British commanders. In 1908 he became the first Canadian to command the nation's military forces. He retired in 1910. However, he came out of retirement during the First World War (1914–18) to command internment operations of enemy nationals resident in Canada.

Otter was knighted in 1913. In the aftermath of the First World War he chaired the "Otter Commission," to aid in the continuation of Canadian Expeditionary Force units that served overseas. He was promoted to general in 1923. Otter died on May 6, 1929.

The fact that Otter was the interim commandant of Belmont Station did not help matters. His seemingly preoccupation with garrison duties and mundane training created resentment. The eventual arrival of the British appointed commandant, Lieutenant-Colonel Thomas Pilcher, just enflamed the problem. Within his first week, Pilcher organized a flying column that included "C" Company, The RCR, and launched a highly successful strike against a group of Boers who were conducting operations near the town of Douglas.

IMPORTANT FACTS

Kopje

Kopje is the term used to describe an isolated granite formation, such as a rock hill, ridge, or small mountain that rises abruptly from the level surrounding veldt in southern Africa. Kopje is originally a Dutch word from which the Afrikaans term koppie was derived.

On January 1, 1900, Pilcher's flying column surprised the Boers at Sunnyside Kopje. As the artillery shelled the unprepared enemy, the Royal Canadians seized a small kopje, 1,200 metres from the enemy position, and opened fire on the Boers. As the other British forces closed the noose on the Boers, the Canadians advanced on the enemy position, closing to approximately 200 metres and awaiting the order to charge. However, after four hours of fighting and being almost totally surrounded, the Boers fled toward Douglas. The fight had been a great success. The small British force had killed six enemy, wounded 12, and captured 34.

This engagement represented the first experience under fire for the Canadians, yet they seemed to have conducted themselves well. "Although the fire of the Boers was apparently very hot for a time," reported Otter, "LCol Pilcher who commanded the flying column … speaks very highly of the steadiness under fire and general good conduct of the Royal Canadians during this special service."

The attack at Sunnyside simply increased the grousing. It was not lost on The RCR soldiers that Pilcher, even though he had just

The Battle of Ridgeway

The Battle of Ridgeway was fought on June 2, 1866, near the town of Fort Erie, Ontario. The battle occurred when the town was raided by Fenians.

The Fenian brotherhood was established in Ireland in 1858, in order to free Ireland from British rule and establish the Republic of Ireland. John O'Mahony, leader of the U.S. branch, thought that a Fenian occupied Canada could be traded for a free Ireland.

Approximately 1,000 Fenians crossed the border and occupied Fort Erie on June 1, 1866. That night they marched to present-day Ridgeway. The next morning approximately 850 Canadian militiamen attacked. At first the Canadians seemed to be winning, but the tide quickly turned and the Fenians chased the Canadians off the battlefield with bayonets. The Fenians then burned the town of Ridgeway to the ground and withdrew to Fort Erie. Nine Canadians were killed and approximately 37 were wounded. The Fenian casualties were unknown, although Canadian sources stated that at least six were killed.

The Canadian defeat was embarrassing but not surprising. Compared to the battle-hardened war veterans serving with the Fenians, very few of the Canadian militia troops had actually practiced firing live rounds.

The Fenian force defeated another smaller Canadian contingent (a company of the Canadian volunteer Welland Field Battery and the Dunnville Naval Brigade) later that day in Fort Erie. However, realizing that a large reinforcement of British regular troops was on the way, the Fenians quickly withdrew across the river to return to the United States.

become commandant of Belmont Station, spent his time planning and conducting offensive operations instead of doing administrative tasks. Not surprisingly, the criticisms of Otter continued and grew.

But the expectations of the soldiers were somewhat misguided as well. Their inexperience could be fatal. Otter's memories of the fight at Ridgeway in 1866 against the Fenians, and later combat in the North-West Rebellion in 1885, taught him the importance of drill, discipline, and fitness. His emphasis on marching and battle drill, specifically the new "rushing tactics" that stemmed from the lessons of the defeats of Black Week, was instrumental in preparing the Royal Canadians for their upcoming campaign. So were the occasional forays into the outlying areas on reconnaissance. These activities improved the physical endurance of the troops and gave them experience in operating in the harsh environment, as well as a better knowledge of the country and terrain. As late as February 11, Otter noted, "I confess to being somewhat disappointed in the condition of many of the men ... I find that there are many who it is unsafe to put upon any extra strain for the reason that they are constitutionally unable to meet it." Therefore, this initial period, as monotonous as it may have seemed, was instrumental in preparing the men for what lay ahead.

IMPORTANT FACTS

The North-West Rebellion

The North-West Rebellion was a short and unsuccessful upris-ing by the Métis and First Nations of the current province of Saskatchewan in 1885. The Métis and Native peoples were frustrated with the increased settlement of their lands and the reduction of the buffalo herds. Although they appealed to the government to protect their rights and land, little was done. In 1884, Louis Riel took up their cause, as he had done in 1869–70 during the Red River Rebellion in Manitoba. On March 8, 1885, Riel called a meeting and passed a 10-point "Revolutionary Bill of Rights," for the Métis. Ten days later Riel announced the creation of a provisional government under his control, which included its own armed force held at Batoche. Riel sent a force to Duck Lake, midway between Batoche and the North-West Mounted Police (NWMP) garrison at Fort Carlton. On the morning of March 26, 1885, Riel's force engaged the NWMP force. After a short skirmish, the NWMP force withdrew. In total, nine vol-unteers and three police were killed. Riel's group lost six dead.

Using the new CPR rail line, the government dispatched approximately 3,000 troops to the west to reinforce the 1,700 men already stationed there, giving Major-General Frederick Middleton, the commanding general, almost 5,000 soldiers.

Throughout that spring and summer many battles and skir-mishes were fought. In the end, the government forces prevailed. By the end of August, the Canadian troops sent to put down the rebellion had returned home.

Louis Riel was tried for treason in front of a jury of his peers. He was found guilty and sentenced to death by hanging. His execution was postponed three times to allow for appeals and to determine his level of sanity. However, Riel was hanged at Regina on November 16, 1885. As for the Native key leaders, Poundmaker and Big Bear were also tried and sentenced to three years in prison.

The adage "be careful what you wish for" never rang more true. The Battalion clamoured for action and they would soon realize their wish. On February 12, 1900, the Battalion moved to Graspan and joined the 19th Brigade under Major-General Horace Smith-Dorrien. The Battalion now began an epic campaign. Lord Robert's army of 35,000 men was set to march to Bloemfontein, which would effec-tively relieve the siege of Kimberley and Ladysmith since it would force the withdrawal of the besieging Boer armies from their positions of vantage in Natal and Cape Colony or risk themselves being cut-off and surrounded. The march, however, would be done without railway support. This necessitated the bare minimum of supplies. Tents, extra equipment, and all other superfluous materials were left behind.

FROM THE INTELLIGENCE FILES

Winston Churchill

Sir Winston Leonard Spencer-Churchill was an adventurer, artist, military officer, journalist, politician, and statesman. He is best known for his leadership of the United Kingdom during the Second World War, when he served as the British prime minister. He was born the aristocratic family of the Duke of Marlborough on November 30, 1874. As a junior officer in the British Army, he participated in combat in India, the Sudan, and the Second Anglo-Boer War, where he was captured by the Boers and later escaped. He became a well-known writer and war correspondent as a result of his writings about the campaigns that he both witnessed and participated in. In fact, he remains the only British prime minister to have been awarded the Nobel Prize in Literature. However, he is most well known for his achievements during his fifty years in politics. He held various key positions during peace and both world wars.

Churchill, who died on January 24, 1965, is considered among the most influential men in British history.

LAC, PA-181416.

Rail move to the front. Note how the soldiers were packed into open rail cars.

CHAPTER 3

Death on the Veldt

THE MARCH OF THE RCR, WHICH NOW NUMBERED 31 OFFICERS AND 865 other ranks, commenced on February 13, 1900. The first three days were difficult. Although they only marched an average of 19 kilometres a day, the hot climate, difficult terrain, and extra fatigue duties they had to perform each day, such as assisting heavy naval guns cross rivers, took its toll. Adding to the misery was the Boer capture of a convoy of 200 British supply wagons on the morning of February 15. This meant that everyone, despite the very difficult conditions, would be on short rations for the foreseeable future.

The next day the Battalion moved into Jacobsdal and remained there during the day. Due to the excessive heat, the troops resumed marching at night. That evening, at 2100 hours, the Battalion departed for Klipdrift on the Modder River. Seven hours later they arrived at their objective and rested until 1800 hours that night, when they set off once again for Paardeberg Drift. At 0600 hours, on February 18, the Royal Canadians arrived at their destination, extremely fatigued and famished. Arrangements were immediately made for a much-anticipated breakfast, despite the meagre rations available.

The meal was barely started when shots rang out in the distance. The British field force had caught General Piet Cronjé's army of 5,000 Boer troops on the Modder River. The hunter had become the hunted. The Boer army that had just recently besieged Kimberley was now trapped. The RCR were ordered to dislodge or capture them. By 0720 hours, the Royal Canadians, most without a meal, deployed from their lines.

The troops were not impressed. "The state of many of the men was now pitiable," reported one embedded journalist. "The short rations, want of water, lack of sleep, and long, tedious and irregular marches had told on them…. Others were chafed and bleeding with the sand … we threw ourselves down half-dead and were just in

RCR soldiers crossing the swift-flowing Modder River at Paardeberg Drift, February 18, 1900.

Photographer Reinhold Thiele, LAC, C-014923.

the act of getting breakfast, when the order came that we were to form for the attack."

The perspective of the soldiers was not much different. "We were pretty well fatigued as we had not slept or ate or even had a drink of water since yesterday," scribbled Lance-Corporal John Kennedy Hill in his diary. Another account reinforced the state of exhaustion. "On the night of the 17th we made a forced march (about 23 miles) arriving on the scene at daybreak," recorded Private F. Dunham in his diary. "We thought that before we went into action we should receive some food to fill our shrunken stomachs but no, we had hardly halted when we were ordered to wade the Modder [river] & attack the N[orth] side."

The river proved to be a formidable obstacle. It was five feet deep and the current ran at approximately 24 kilometres-per-hour. Ropes were strung from bank to bank to assist with the crossing, but to speed up the process groups of four men linked arms and struck for the opposite side. "We did wade across that swiftly flowing river right up to our necks, four abreast," explained Dunham. "If one slipped he was supported by his comrades. Thus we gained the opposite bank." Lance-Corporal John Kennedy Hill, in a timeless understatement, recounted, "We had quite a time crossing as water was up to our chins and current very strong."

FROM THE INTELLIGENCE FILES

General Piet Cronjé

General Piet Cronjé, formally known as Pieter Arnoldus Cronjé, was born in Cape Colony on October 4, 1836. His family left Cape Colony and Cronjé was raised in the Transvaal. Renowned for his courage, he established his reputation in the First Anglo-Boer War in 1880–81, when he led the siege of the British garrison at Potchefstroom. He was also in command of the force that caught Dr. Leander Starr Jameson, who led the ill-fated Jameson raid in 1896. Jameson, with the knowledge of members of the British government, attempted to lead a private army from a neighbouring state to overthrow the Boer government in the Transvaal. Cronjé rounded up Jameson and his force at Doornkop on January 2, 1896.

During the second Anglo-Boer War of 1899–1902, Cronjé was the Boer general commanding in the western theatre of the war. He began the sieges of Kimberley and Mafeking. He scored a brilliant victory against the British at the Battle of the Modder River, one of the three battles later to be called "Black Week" by the British. He was eventually defeated at the Battle of Paardeberg, where he surrendered with 4,150 of his soldiers on February 27, 1900, after being surrounded by British forces. After his surrender, the British sent him to St. Helena Island as a prisoner of war. He remained there until the war was over in 1902.

On the other side the men were immediately deployed into extended order in the direction of the Boer positions. By 0930 hours, the Battalion was firm on the other bank and began what would be nine days of fighting for Paardeberg Drift. Their baptism of fire was a true test of their mettle. Dunham wrote in his journal:

> This was the first time [February 18] our Regiment as a whole were engaged.... Within 1,800 yards of their position the bullets began to hum around.... But nothing daunted us as we kept steadily marching forward.

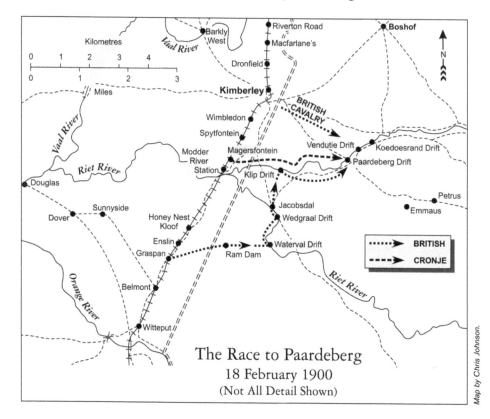

The Race to Paardeberg
18 February 1900
(Not All Detail Shown)

Map by Chris Johnson.

A sort of wild excitement to be at them came upon us so we hastened forward…. Within 800 yards we supported the front or firing line. Things began to be rather hot so we adopted the rushing tactics, that is running fifty yards then lying down for a few minutes for breath and again pushing on. This we kept up to within 450 yards for the fire was too hot and their aim too sure. Here we lay for several hours keeping up a hot fire all the time. The sun showed no mercy on us. Instead it seemed to shine with greater fierceness so that the sweat rolled from us as it never rolled before.

The Battalion advanced with "A," "B," and "C" Companies in the forward firing line under Lieutenant-Colonel Lawrence Buchan, the Battalion second-in-command (2IC). "D" and "E" Companies were in support and the remainder in reserve. They were flanked by the Duke of Cornwall's Light Infantry (Cornwalls) on the right (but on the other side of the river) and the King's Own Shropshire Light Infantry (Shropshires) and Gordon Highlanders on the left.

Not surprisingly, there was a lot of confusion on the battlefield. "The bullets were whizzing past us, and throwing little sprays of sand in all directions as they struck the ground," recalled Sergeant W. Hart-McHarg. "In a very few minutes we were well in the fire zone, and were ordered to lie down." He quickly observed that all around them were men of the other British regiments. The advance continued until the Royal Canadians reached the forward firing line, where they intermingled with the British regulars. Often men could not fire at the Boers for fear of hitting their comrades who were in the line fire.

Battles of the 19th Century, 1902.

An artist's conception of the advance against the Boer positions at Paardeberg.

FROM THE INTELLIGENCE FILES

Letter from an Officer

The following letter was written by an officer at Paardeberg Drift on February 26, 1900, and sent to his family:

The Battalion arrived near Paardeberg Drift with the 19th Brigade at 6 A.M. on the 8th having formed the rear guard to the brigade in its march during the night from Klip drift, a distance of 22 miles.

Within half an hour on the arrival of the battalion orders were received to be ready on parade at 7 A.M. The battalion moved out to support the artillery about a mile away…. The companies as they crossed were pushed forward, and at 10 A.M. A and C Cos. under Captains Arnold and Barker, were in the firing line at about 1,800 yards from the enemy, who occupied the woods along the near edge of the river but were totally hidden from view. They also occupied a series of dongas enfilading our left flank but this was not discovered until the afternoon when they disclosed themselves – although they were quietly snipping from that direction all day.

Firing began about 9:30 A.M. from the enemy's left at long range and continued along their front toward the centre. The advance of the battalion too [sic] place over perfectly open ground, somewhat undulating, and with no cover save the inequalities of the ground and a few ant hills.

Only one maxim gun could be crossed and that was soon got into position by Capt. Bell on the rising ground to the left at a distance of some 1,000 yards where it did most excellent service during the day, being in a position to keep down the fire of the enemy who occupied the dongas on our left. A battery of field artillery occupied the hill on our left rear and shelled the enemy's lines at intervals during the day. The fire discipline of the several companies engaged was excellent, and perfect coolness as well as accurate shooting were maintained.

Author photo.

Brass relief on the Boer War memorial in Montreal depicting the Battle of Paardeberg.

Once the Canadians reached the firing line the advance came to a grinding halt. The Boer fire was simply too overwhelming. Their accurate and smooth-firing bolt-action Mauser rifles cracked ceaselessly at any target that showed itself. "We lay in the burning sun, under the cover of small bushes or anthills, or lying flat on the open, jamming ourselves into the very ground to escape the peppering hail of bullets which ripped, whirred, and whinged a continual chorus of malignant warning," recounted one participant. Private Gerald Cadogen remembered, "As we crept nearer the firing line I became aware of the fact that I was trying to dodge the unseen bullets that were whistling past my ears by jerking my head from side to side."

The Royal Canadians were now strung out in front of the Boer positions from approximately 400 metres on the right to 700 metres on the left, the difference owing to the terrain that allowed the troops on the right more cover. Many, overcome with fatigue and feeling the effects of the relentless burning sun, fell asleep clinging to the ground or behind whatever scanty cover they could find. Some died this way — the target of Boer marksman who continued to shoot at any target they could locate. The official battalion report noted: "The enemy's fire was … delivered when the least exposure was made by our men … on our part the fire discipline was excellent, the men being cool and collected, but they laboured under the difficulty of fighting an invisible enemy."

"We lay in the open," recalled Private Cadogen, "exposed to a most galling fire and without cover of any sort…. I remember the order as we opened fire — not at the enemy mind you — but at the line of trees in front at six hundred yards commence firing — yes a paltry

FROM THE WEAPONS LOCKER

The Mauser Rifle

Mauser was a German arms manufacturer that produced a line of high-quality bolt-action rifles from the 1870s until 1995.

Peter Paul Mauser, the designer of the Mauser rifle, was born on June 27, 1838. He was the son of a gunsmith. In 1859, he was conscripted into the military as an artillery-man at the Ludwigsburg arsenal, where he worked as a gunsmith. Here he developed a rifle with a turn-bolt mechanism that cocked the gun as the user pulled the trigger. At first the rifle used a firing needle, adapted from the Dreyse needle gun, but later Mauser developed a version that used a firing pin and a cartridge with a rear-ignition primer.

The Mauser rifle was accepted by the Prussian government on December 2, 1871. Variations of the Mauser rifle were used by the German army in both the First and Second World Wars. The Mauser rifle was also the small arm of choice for the Boers, due to its smooth firing action, accuracy, and dependability.

five hundred yards separated us from the enemy but I am prepared to swear on a stack of bibles — that I lay for five hours firing at those bless trees without ever seeing a Boer." He asserted it was perhaps "a waste of ammunition … perhaps not — as we afterward found out the Boer trenches lay right under those very trees." But the return fire from the Boers was hot.

Cadogen recalled:

> Ah a close call that, as I wipe some of the sand out of my eyes — and a Mauser bullet buries itself in the loose sand a few inches from my chin — and I grip my rifle — as the only thing to be cherished — the atmosphere in front of me has turned a livid red — have you ever witnessed that extraordinary phenomenon, God grant you never will — the lust of vengeance took possession of my being — I longed to kill — and almost as thought came — my rifle spoke for the first time — and the bullet sped on its way — accompanied by my heartfelt wish — I hope you will find a berth in the fatty part of some Boer's anatomy, and almost as an answer a bullet zipped past my ear.

At 1530 hours a brief thunderstorm drenched the pinned-down soldiers, providing some relief. But the storm seemed almost an omen for the tempest that would shortly engulf the Royal Canadians. Approximately 30 minutes later the commanding officer of the Cornwalls, Lieutenant-Colonel William Aldworth, who had been ordered by Lord Kitchener to "finish this thing," arrived on the battlefield. After a very brief and unpleasant discussion with Otter he

Canadian Military Museum, Bacon's South African Battle Pictures, No. 10, 1900.

"proposed going in with bayonet." He then ordered three of his companies across the river and moved them forward to the firing line. At approximately 1715 hours, after "offering five pounds to the first man in the enemy's trenches," Aldworth ordered his men to charge and "invited" all others from the wide array of gathered regiments to join them. The effect was electric. Along the whole line the intermingled

This contemporary drawing, **Dashing Advance of the Canadians at Paardeberg,** *is utterly inaccurate, however, it does capture the excitement and public image of the battle.*

soldiers of the various regiments, who had been paralyzed by inactivity, were seized by the sudden excitement. The Canadians were no different and immediately rose and joined the charge.

"It was about 4:30 in the afternoon that the order passed along the line like a thunderbolt to 'fix bayonets,'" recalled Private Dunham. "Never for a moment did we flinch, so when the order came to prepare to charge we jumped to our feet with a stifled cheer & charged." Excitement and enthusiasm, however, were not enough. "And, oh! That wild, mad charge against an invisible enemy," explained Reverend O'Leary. "Hell let loose would give but a faint idea of it."

In a letter to his aunt, Private Jesse Biggs described:

> We got the order to charge. Then there was a rain of bullets. The Boers seemed to have waited for our customary charge and kept their magazines loaded in anticipation, then they certainly did turn loose on us.

Had those on the ground been questioned, every one of them would have answered that a charge was a very foolish idea. "When we started to move," recalled Lieutenant J.C. Mason, "the bullets fell like a perfect hailstorm." One journalist wrote, "The men tumbled like skittles on every side." Private Dunham explained, "It was too hot for us; we were compelled to stop." Another participant watched as the enemy "opened a fearful fire on us which compelled us to lie down again and take cover as to advance … would have been mere madness and could have done no good." Both Mason and Dunham agreed it was an unnecessary act. Mason felt that "it was a hopeless undertaking to cover 600 yards of open ground when the enemy had the exact range," and Dunham wrote that "the order to charge was another of those blunderings which cost our army so dear." The brigade commander, Major-General Smith-Dorrien, later told his troops he had not ordered the charge — which was the truth.

The charge occurred nonetheless. Lieutenant-Colonel Aldworth was one of the first to be killed in the ill-fated assault. In the end, the British and Canadian troops only gained another 182 metres. At that point the soldiers were once again forced to fling themselves to the ground and desperately attempt to melt into any available crack and crevice to avoid the deadly reach of the Mauser bullets.

The Royals were in a desperate spot. "I stayed out on the battlefield right under the Boer trenches with a poor fellow who had been shot in the throat," wrote Richard Thompson to his brother. "It is marvellous how I escaped as my helmet was shot off my head...." Another soldier lamented, "It is something awful the rattle of the fire and the moans of the dying."

Darkness became their only hope and salvation. At about 1900 hours, once the battlefield was cloaked in darkness, Otter gave the order to withdraw. "Within a few hundred yards of the enemy we lay till night closed around us, then quietly retired," scribbled

FROM THE WEAPONS LOCKER

The Lee-Enfield Rifle

The Lee-Enfield bolt-action rifle was the small arm that was issued to all infantrymen in the British Army from 1895 until it was taken out of service in 1957. The rifle used the .303 British cartridge and was magazine fed, and was a redesigned version of the Lee-Metford rifle that had been adopted by the British Army in 1888. The Lee-Enfield rifle takes the first part of its name from the designer of the rifle's bolt action system, James Paris *Lee*. The second part is taken from the factory where it was designed, the Royal Small Arms Factory in *Enfield*, England.

The rifle's detachable metal, 10-round, double-column magazine was a very modern development at the time. The very conservative British Army leadership was originally opposed to the idea of a detachable magazine. They worried that the private soldier would lose the magazine during operations. However, the quick-operating bolt action rifle and large magazine capacity allowed a great volume of rounds to be fired in a short period of time. In fact, a well-trained rifleman could fire 20 to 30 rounds in a minute for short periods of time, making the Lee-Enfield rifle the fastest military bolt-action rifle of the period. The Lee-Enfield went on to see service in both the First and Second World Wars. The Canadian Rangers in the Arctic are still issued the Lee-Enfield IV rifle today. It is estimated that a total of 17 million Lee-Enfield rifles have been produced.

Dunham in his diary. "It was a sad moment for us, to leave the ground we had so dearly won." The day's action cost the Battalion 21 killed and 60 wounded.

Although darkness provided a reprieve, it was clear to all that the Battalion had been blooded. Private Bennett summed up the day:

> On the 18th we had our first fight, and that was the hottest fought on this side.... We marched all the previous night, doing 28 miles, and got here at 5 a.m. We had just got a mouthful of coffee and a ration of rum, when we were ordered out to the field, and from 10 a.m. fought till dark.... The fire was something awful, and some of the Highlanders, who were at Magersfontein, say that the fire was worse here than there.

Bennett described:

> We lay on our stomachs all day in the hot sun, and took a shot whenever we could. The bullets whistled round my head all day but I took good care to keep low and so got through without a wound. I was so tired that I fell asleep several times during the day, and was that way when that rash charge was sounded and so was unable to participate in it, which perhaps was for the good.... I didn't get a chance to fire a shot all day on account of the risk of hitting our own men who were just ahead. We all agree that we have had all the fighting we want, and will be glad to get back to the line of communication as soon as possible.

Private Cadogen had a similar view of events.

> How we marched from 3 pm that afternoon until 6 am next morning [February 18], is by this time ancient history, but the memory of those two days, Saturday and Sunday Feb 17th and 18th 1900 are always with me sleeping or waking…. During that time some of the finest specimens of Canadian manhood laid down their young lives for the love of their Queen and the honour of the empire…. Some in awful agony, some painlessly but all unmurmuringly — I with more luck than I deserved escaped with a few bullets through my helmet and haversack…. All I know was — that that morning the humid air reeked with lead and death.

In the end the Royals, who had come for adventure, who sought "action," saw war's grim side. "We all agree," wrote one young soldier, "that we have had all the fighting we want, and will be glad to get back to the line of communication as soon as possible."

FROM THE INTELLIGENCE FILES

The Emergency Ration

The Emergency Ration was a cylindrical-shaped article that contained a quarter pound of concentrated essence of beef and a quarter pound of chocolate. Soldiers were told that they should endeavour to digest their haversack, water bottle, and helmet before touching their emergency ration.

On February 19, 1900, at 0130 hours, a Private Gerald Cadogan on the field of battle, among the dead and dying, after 34½ hours without eating, marching for 50 kilometres, and fighting for 14 hours, began to feel weak with hunger and ate his emergency ration. He was later tried and convicted for eating his emergency ration without proper authorization.

CHAPTER 4

Finishing Business

DESPITE THE UNSUCCESSFUL ASSAULT, THE BRITISH HAD SOME SUCCESS. At nightfall the Boers withdrew to better a defensive position. But Cronjé's large army was completely surrounded by an overwhelming British force. The trap was strong enough that he could not break out, nor could Boer reinforcements relieve the pressure or save him. The siege continued with both the British and Boers manning entrenchments and harassing the other with artillery and small-arms fire.

The Royal Canadians took their turn manning both outposts and the main entrenchment facing the Boers. On February 19, 1900, the Battalion buried its dead and manned a series of outposts five kilometres up river, approximately 3,500 metres from the Boer laager. Two days later The RCR were sent to Artillery Hill to support the naval guns that were shelling the Boers with lyddite (high explosives). The Royals also manned a series of outposts at night. On the 22nd they were relieved, but the arrival of a large Boer force that intended to break the siege meant that the Royals were reassigned with the remainder of 19th Brigade to man a line of kopjes to the west as

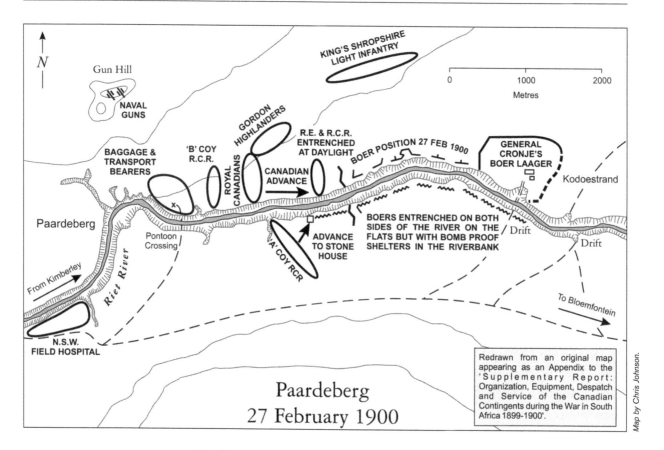

Paardeberg
27 February 1900

Redrawn from an original map appearing as an Appendix to the 'Supplementary Report: Organization, Equipment, Despatch and Service of the Canadian Contingents during the War in South Africa 1899-1900'.

Map by Chris Johnson.

a blocking force. On the 24th, after three days of heavy rain, the Battalion was sent back to Paardeberg Drift for a rest. This proved to be of little value as the torrential rains continued throughout the night, turning their camp into a quagmire.

The mud was the least of their concerns. The heavy rains caused the river, which ran through their camp and was the only source of drinking water, to flood. The swift current that also ran through the Boer laager carried the debris of the besieged camp — specifically its dead and its waste. Otter reported that the greater part of their "rest day" was spent polling off dead men and animals from the banks of their camp to prevent them from creating a dam. In the brief 24-hour period spent in the camp, Otter estimated that a minimum of 720 bodies and carcasses drifted down from the Boer laager. This fouled the drinking supply, creating serious problems in the form of enteric and typhoid fever that eventually affected 350 men in the Battalion, 10 percent of whom would die from disease.

On the morning of February 26, the Battalion was ordered into the trenches to relieve some British troops. The entrenchments were gradually being pushed toward the enemy position. When the Royal Canadians arrived they found themselves approximately 600 metres from the Boer lines. For the remainder of the day the Canadians engaged the Boers with small-arms fire. All hoped for an end to the siege and most felt that the end was near. "At present we are surrounding Cronjé and his force, and now have them cooped up like rats in a hole, though it has been at a great cost," wrote one participant. "We are shelling them continually with shrapnel and lyddite, and they are readily famished, as we have learned from prisoners and almost ready to surrender."

FROM THE WEAPONS LOCKER

Lyddite

Lyddite was a form of high explosive widely used during the Boer War. It was named after the location in southern England where the secret trials to test its effectiveness were done. Lyddite was first tested in 1888, and proved to be very effective. Combined with armour-piercing shells, the lyddite detonated while the shell was tearing through the armour. The explosive was composed of molten and cast picric acid, which is a yellow crystalline chemical compound. Lyddite was used extensively during the Battle of Paardeberg to destroy the Boer entrenchments and encampment, as well as kill men and livestock. It was also very effective at destroying Boer morale.

Battles of the 19th Century, 1902.

The shelling of the Boer positions at Paardeberg.

FROM THE WEAPONS LOCKER

The "Pom-Pom" Gun

"Pom-Pom" is a nickname given to the Maxim-Nordenfelt quick-firing 1-pounder auto-cannon and the Vickers-Maxim 37-mm infantry gun used during the Second Anglo-Boer War. It derived its nickname from the sound that the guns made – "pom-pom-pom." The gun was designed in the 1880s by the famous machine-gun developer, Hiram Maxim. He originally designed the Pom-Pom as a larger version of his Maxim machine gun. At first, the British government rejected the gun. However, the South African Republic (Transvaal), as well as other countries purchased it. Ironically, British troops in South Africa quickly found themselves coming under accurate fire from the British-designed auto-cannons. As a result, the British government purchased a large number from Vickers-Maxim and had them shipped into theatre. The first three arrived in time to take part in the Battle of Paardeberg. They were effective in bombarding the Boer encampment and entrenchments.

LAC, PA-185349.

Boer dugouts at Paardeberg.

With such a turn of events the British commanders decided to put additional pressure on the Boers. That afternoon the Battalion received word that a night attack, at 0200 hours, would be conducted. Preparations were made and the Battalion braced for its second major engagement of the war. The soldiers were not overly enthusiastic. "Nothing is so trying on the nerves as a night attack," Private Dunham wrote in his diary, "and we had lots of time to ponder on it."

The plan of attack was for six RCR companies in the main trench (i.e., "C," "D", "E," "F," "G," and "H" companies) to advance on the Boer trenches at the assigned hour. In the main trench to the right of The RCRs were 200 Gordon Highlanders. To the left, approximately 1,500 metres away, were the Shropshire Light Infantry. These battalions were to provide covering fire if needed. For the assaulting Royal Canadians, the front rank of each company was to move with fixed bayonets and they were not to fire until fired upon by the enemy. The rear rank, with engineer support, was to sling their rifles and carry shovels and picks that they would use to entrench. Once the advance ground to a stop and could go no further, the rear rank, supported by the fire of the front rank and adjacent units, was to dig-in.

FROM THE WEAPONS LOCKER

Shrapnel

Shrapnel refers to the fragments of metal that are thrown from the casing of an exploding shell. Their hot, jagged iron or steel composition makes them extremely lethal. Shrapnel originally came from shrapnel shells, which were specially made to contain a large number of individual projectiles that would be launched close to a target. The shell would eject the projectiles, which would continue along the original shell's trajectory and strike the target in a large wave of individual "shrapnel."

The name is taken from the creator of the first shrapnel shell, British Major-General Henry Shrapnel. The shrapnel shell became obsolete at the end of the First World War when the high-explosive fragmenting shell was developed.

FROM THE INTELLIGENCE FILES

The Dawn of Majuba

The Battle of Majuba Hill took place during the first Anglo-Boer War, on the night of February 27, 1881, near Volksrust, South Africa. Major-General Sir George Pomeroy Colley had led a night march on February 26, with approximately 400 men, to the top of Majuba Hill overlooking the main Boer position at Laing's Nek. He had hoped to outflank the Boers and force them to withdraw from their position. However, once the Boers realized that the British had seized the dominating height they quickly assaulted the British position. Using the scrub and vegetation as cover for concealment, they advanced stealthily and used their superior marksmanship to snipe at the exposed British soldiers while other stormed parts of the hill and drove off the British. Under the relentless assault, and seeing even more Boers encircling the mountain, the British discipline broke and soldiers began to retreat, which soon turned into panic. As a result, the Boers were able to inflict heavy casualties on the British troops. Approximately 280 British soldiers were killed, captured, or wounded compared to the Boers who suffered one dead and five wounded. The battle led to the signing of a peace treaty that ended the war and to the Pretoria Convention between the England and the newly created South African Republic. During the Second Anglo-Boer War, the British used the slogan "Remember Majuba" to rally their troops.

At 0215 hours, in the inky Transvaal darkness, the Royal Canadians crept out of their entrenchments and moved forward. They maintained an interval of one pace between men and a distance of 15 paces between ranks. Initially the advance seemed too good to be true. The front rank moved forward without interruption for about 400 metres. Then, suddenly, a few stray shots rang out and then a terrific fire engulfed the darkness. Luckily the initial shots served as a warning and many of the soldiers threw themselves down to the ground before the flame of fire erupted. "Silently we advanced for several hundred yards, then the order came to ease off to the left," explained Private Dunham. "We hardly had moved two steps when a wall of fire opened up in front of us, not fifty yards

LAC, PA-C-6399.

RCR soldiers rummaging through the spoils of the captured Boer position at Paardeberg.

LAC, PA 24627.

Canadian soldiers guard Boer prisoners.

away and a hail of bullets whizzed past us, sending death with it…. We all dropped as flat as pancakes and lay there while the fusillade lasted."

But not all were so lucky. "Now we are in for it and no mistake," reflected Gerald Carogan. "Crossfire everywhere the Boers are only 100 yards from us now but, there is a solid wall of lead between us and them — the hail of lead is pouring in on us from every side … in our ranks men are dropping on every side — hundred be dead or dying in our wake, and hundreds more must die before those trenches are reached — but no its impossible — no human being can move against that hail of lead."

Another participant recalled, "The first news we had of the enemy was a sheet of flame not twenty yards away." Private Bennett wrote, "I don't see how we came through at all … we hadn't gained more than 450 yards when the enemy opened fire at 50 yards, killing and wounding several. The fire was awfully hot." The noise of the battle impressed Private William Jeffery. "The explosive bullets sounded like flying devils hissing and smacking through the air." One journalist who witnessed the event described it as "a brief fight, but a long half hour of deadly combat." He added, "Ten minutes of triple hell and twenty minutes of an ordinary inferno." The Boer volley had a disastrous effect on "F" and "G" companies, which were caught in the open within 60 metres of the enemy's advanced trench. Combined they suffered six killed and 21 wounded in mere minutes. Private Perkins wrote, "How we got back is a wonder to us all. It was like being in a swarm of bees."

The assaulting Canadians in the front rank hugged the ground and returned fire. They were supported by the Shropshires, who unleashed volleys of fire from their distant entrenchments in a vain effort to provide covering fire and distract the Boers. The rear rank of the Royal Canadians began to entrench, but progress was mixed. The trench on the right, being constructed by Royal Engineers (RE)

Battles of the 19th Century, 1902.

Artist conception of General Cronjé surrendering to the British commander.

IMPORTANT FACTS

The Victoria Cross

The Victoria Cross (VC) was established on January 29, 1856, as the highest British military decoration for valour "in the face of the enemy." All members of the armed forces of the British Empire, later Commonwealth countries, were eligible to be awarded the VC. It can be awarded to a military member of any rank and takes precedence over all other orders, decorations, and medals. The VC was established in 1856 by Queen Victoria, who wished to honour the gallantry of military members during the Crimean War. In total, 1,356 VCs have been awarded, to 1,353 individuals, since its creation. The last VC was awarded in July 2007 for bravery during combat in Afghanistan.

who "worked liked demons" and supported by "G" and "H" companies, made rapid progress and was approximately 100 metres from the enemy position. The trenches on the left were not doing as well.

The fog of war took hold of the battlefield. In the murky darkness, amidst the carnage, death, and fear in battle, an authoritative voice ordered all "to retire and bring back your wounded." The apparent directive was enough for most — the entire left side of the line, four companies in total, collapsed in a rush to the rear, back to the main trench. "I think all records for the 100 yards were broken that night," penned Private Dunham.

The precipitous withdrawal angered Otter. The hasty retreat put the reputation of the Canadians at risk. Conscious of the disdain that the British regulars held for colonials, Otter was concerned this would simply reinforce their perceptions. However, fate smiled on The RCR that night. Daylight found "G" and "H" Companies well entrenched, with the Royal Engineers still pushing on with their work. It has never become clear whether the tenacious troops were oblivious to the supposed order and general withdrawal that took place in the dark, or whether strong local leadership took over. Either way, at 0400 hours, as the light of dawn slowly seeped onto the battlefield, the Boers rose from their trenches to investigate their night's work. Suddenly the tables were turned. They came under fire from the newly constructed trench less than 100 metres from their position.

IMPORTANT FACTS

The Queen's Scarves

In recognition of the service and sacrifice of her soldiers during the Boer War, Queen Victoria crocheted eight khaki-coloured Berlin-wool scarves, each about 2.4 metres long by 20 centimetres wide. She shipped four of the scarves to Field Marshal Roberts, the commander-in-chief of the South African Field Force.

The "Canadian scarf" was awarded to Private Richard Rowland for his bravery on the battlefield. Details are given in a separate sidebar.

Queen Victoria sent another four scarves to her grandson, Major Prince Christian Victor, so that he could award them to members of the British Regular Army as well. The prince, aware of the tribulations involved with selecting the "worthy" recipients, simply forwarded one scarf to each of the four British regular force battalions of the 2nd Brigade, the formation he served with before being transferred to 5 Division Headquarters. He left the difficult task of choosing the worthy individual to the battalion commanders. In the end, each of the battalions awarded their respective scarf to a colour sergeant, the senior non-commissioned officer serving in a rifle company.

Although the scarves were a great honour, British authorities clearly stated that the award of a Queen's scarf was a singular achievement and did not imply, or justify, the award of a Victoria Cross (VC). As such, the scarves represented simply a gift and had no status as a gallantry award.

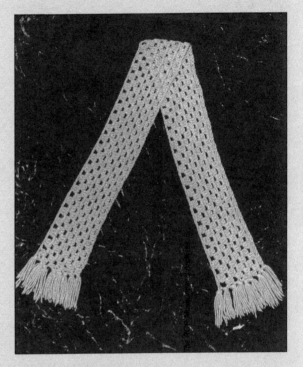

The Queen's Scarf.

At the same time, in the shadows of dawn, an officer spotted a wounded man in the field and called for a volunteer to assist in bringing him in. Without hesitation, Private Thompson went to the aid of a fellow soldier with complete disregard for the danger. He dropped his rifle and ran 275 metres, under fire, to the help the unknown individual. He arrived just before the wounded man was killed by another bullet. Thompson was recommended for the Victoria Cross

FROM THE INTELLIGENCE FILES

White Flag

The white flag is an internationally recognized symbol to designate a truce, ceasefire, or surrender. It also implies a request to parley or negotiate. Importantly, a white flag signifies that the bearer is unarmed and is either surrendering or approaching to negotiate terms of a surrender or ceasefire, or conduct an exchange or some other activity that is beneficial to both parties (e.g., evacuate the dead or wounded from the battlefield). By convention, those carrying a white flag should not be fired on. Those carrying a white flag should not undertake any hostile action either. The use of the white flag to surrender has been enshrined in the Hague Convention on the conduct of war. For this reason, the improper use of a white flag is against the rules of war and is considered a war crime. The flag can be constructed of any available white material or cloth. The first known use of the white flag to surrender has been traced back to both the Eastern Han Dynasty (A.D. 25–220) and the Roman Empire in A.D. 109.

FROM THE INTELLIGENCE FILES

Private Richard Rowland Thompson

Private Richard Rowland was born in Cork, Ireland, in 1877. He studied at Queen's College in Cork for a medical degree but never finished his schooling. He immigrated to Canada and lived in Ottawa. At the outbreak of the Second Boer War he quickly volunteered for duty as a medical assistant and served in "D" Company, 2nd (Special Service) Battalion, The RCR. At the Battle of Paardeberg, Thompson demonstrated extraordinary courage by exposing himself to fire while helping others. On February 18, 1900, he lay in the open for seven hours while maintaining pressure on the ruptured jugular vein of Private James L. H. Bradshaw. Nine days later, he crossed over 200 metres of fire swept ground to reach a wounded soldier who had been shot. Thompson's bravery was later recognized when he was selected as a recipient of one of the Queen's Scarves in early July 1900, "after considerable discussion" by a committee made up of his battalion commander, members of the battalion staff, and the company commanders.

(VC) for his selfless acts of courage, but instead, in July 1900, he received one of seven Queen's Scarves, knit by Queen Victoria "for most distinguished private soldiers in the Colonial Forces of Canada, Australia, New Zealand and South Africa."

The firefight continued for over an hour, until a white flag unexpectedly fluttered over the advanced enemy trench. The Boers had had enough. However, the Canadians were very leery since this tactic had been used before as a ruse. They kept up a well-disciplined fire until 0600 hours, when an individual carrying a white flag emerged from the enemy trenches. The firing stopped immediately. Soon, groups of Boers began to flow from their entrenchments.

LAC, PA-24599.

One Canadian veteran of the battle remarked that the Boer prisoners "were certainly a motley crew, old, middle-aged and young, some carrying blankets, and others pots and pans and articles of food."

The battle for Paardeberg was over. By 0615 hours, the division commander, General Sir Henry Colville, arrived and sent an officer into the Boer laager to discuss the terms of surrender — which were unconditional. Despite the questionable night attack, the tenacity of "G" and "H" Companies had not only saved the reputation of the Battalion, but had created the conditions for the first major British

IMPORTANT FACTS

Queen Victoria

Queen Victoria was born on May 24, 1819, the daughter of Prince Edward, Duke of Kent and Strathearn, the fourth son of King George III. At birth, Victoria was fifth in line for the throne after her father and his three older brothers. However, her grandfather and father both died in 1820. When her uncle George IV passed away in 1830, Victoria's only remaining uncle, William IV, became king. On May 24, 1837, Victoria turned 18, making her eligible for the throne once her uncle abdicated or died. Less than a month later, William IV passed away and Victoria became queen of England.

By then the United Kingdom was already an established constitutional monarchy, leaving Victoria with little political power. However, throughout her reign she attempted to influence governmental policy and appointments. To her subjects, she became an icon. She married Prince Albert of Saxe-Coburg and Gotha in 1840 and bore nine children, who all married into aristocracy across Europe. Her reign as queen lasted almost 64 years and was the longest of any other British monarch. She also reigned longer than any other female monarch in history. Her reign covered a period of dramatic political, economic, and social change. It also marked a period of great expansion for the British Empire. She died on January 22, 1901.

victory of the war. It has also been widely recognized as the turning point of the conflict. Moreover, the date of the victory was very significant. Nineteen years earlier to the day, in 1881, the Boers had inflicted a humiliating defeat on the British, and secured their independence. That embarrassment had been avenged.

The reason for the Boers' surrender soon became apparent. They had suffered enough. "The stench and dirt which everywhere pervaded was something fearful and turned one sick," recorded Lance-Corporal Kennedy in his diary. He described "hundreds of cattle, horses lay in every direction.... There were hundreds of carts and wagons of every description containing remnants of provisions and bedding." Private Bennett wrote, "The Boer Laagar was in an awful state when we entered and I wonder they didn't die of disease.... It was literally strewn with dead horses, oxen and sheep ... the stench of the Laager and trenches was something disgusting."

As The RCR soldiers examined the Boer trenches and helped round up the Boer prisoners little did they know the effect they would have in Canada and Britain. Without knowing it, the Royals did Canada proud.

CHAPTER 5

Doing Canada Proud

THE VICTORY WAS A DISTINCTLY CANADIAN ONE. OTTER WROTE:

> The supporting companies of the Gordon Highlanders
> were not engaged, although the trench which pro-
> tected them was subjected to a fairly heavy fire from the
> enemy. The battalion of the Shropshire Light Infantry
> on our left, fired volleys at long ranges for some time
> after our attack developed and materially assisted
> us…. That the duty entailed on the Royal Canadian
> Regiment was most difficult and dangerous no one will
> deny, and though the advance was not so successful at
> all points as was hoped for, yet the final result was a
> complete success, and credit can fairly be claimed by
> the Battalion for such, as it was practically acting alone.

There was no denying that 2 RCR had made Canada proud.
The effects of the battle were quite profound. After the battle of

Paardeberg, Field Marshal Lord Roberts, the British commander-in-chief in South Africa, told survivors that they "had done noble work, and were as good a lot of men as were in the British Army." Roberts went on to say that "Canadian now stands for bravery, dash and courage." Another British general stated, "Those men [Canadians] can go into battle without a leader they have intelligence and resourcefulness enough to lead themselves." Praise poured in from throughout the empire congratulating the Royal Canadians for their "brilliant achievement," "gallant conduct," and "distinguished gallantry."

The success of the Canadian troops and the seemingly international respect they received soon triggered a nationalist outpouring of pride in Canadian military prowess. Even Canadian Prime Minister Wilfrid Laurier, who was initially hesitant to send troops to South Africa, was not immune to exploiting the success in the field. "Is there a man whose bosom did not swell with pride, the pride of pure patriotism, the pride of consciousness?" thundered Laurier in the Canadian House of Commons. "That day [Paardeberg] the fact had been revealed to the world that a new power had arisen in the West."

On February 22, 1900, Prime Minister Laurier made yet another special address. He stated:

> I desire to convey to you and your men the grateful
> thanks of the Government and Parliament of Canada
> for the gallantry displayed on the battlefield. Canada
> warmly appreciated the sacrifice made by her sons
> for the honor of the Empire. The wounded have our
> sympathy and our prayers for speedy recovery. Those
> who have given up their lives will ever be held in
> remembrance by a grateful people.

In light of the successful outcome of the attack, Otter's anger subsided over the actual conduct of the troops during the assault, specifically their unauthorized retreat. For the soldiers, however, the adulation was of little immediate value. What mattered to them was the fact that Cronjé's surrender meant a rest. The next day the Royal Canadians moved eight kilometres up the Modder River to Kodoesrand to join the remainder of the British field force in a concentration area. The Battalion rested there until March 7, 1900.

The break was short. Since the momentum of the war had shifted with the victory at Paardeberg, British commanders wanted to push the Boers hard and move onto Pretoria — their capital. The advance began with an attack on the Boers at Poplar Grove.

Even though they were in reserve, the Royal Canadians still had a lot of tasks. First, they were assigned to provide an escort for the artillery, which had to retreat from accurate enemy fire. After marching for several kilometres, they were sent to join the Highland Brigade that was rapidly moving against the enemy in support of a division-level attack. This meant a 16-kilometre march. Then the Royal Canadians were ordered to seize a series of small kopjes thought to be occupied by the Boers. Luckily the Battalion completed its task

IMPORTANT FACTS

Bloemfontein

Bloemfontein was officially founded in 1846 as a British outpost by Major Henry Douglas Warden in the Transoranje Region. Warden selected the site because it was close to the existing transportation lines, the lack of horse sickness, and the wide open country. The region transformed into the Orange River Sovereignty in 1848 and finally evolved into the Orange Free State in 1854. Bloemfontein became its capital. The British captured the city on March 13, 1900, during the Second Anglo-Boer War. At the end of the war in 1902, Bloemfontein became the capital city of the Free State Province of South Africa. Bloemfontein literally translates from the Dutch to "fountain of flowers."

without heavy fighting, and from the top of Slags Kraal the Royals were able to witness the hasty retreat of the Boer force.

On the morning of March 10, 1900, the final stage of the march against Bloemfontein, the capital of the Orange Free State, began. The advance was made in three columns, with the Royal Canadians as part of the 9th Division in the centre. The march was largely unopposed and the British forces entered Bloemfontein three days later. By then the Battalion had shrunk to 28 officers and 712 men.

The capture of the capital as well as the Orange Free State rail lines meant that the British Army could stop, rest, and recuperate. The campaign so far had been difficult. "All have been called upon for extraordinary exertion, and have had to undergo forced marches, short rations, great wettings, lack of water and sleep, as well as severe and trying fighting," asserted Major-General Smith-Dorrien. "The Royal Canadian Regiment," reported Otter, "had suffered equally with the others in the matter of short rations; all having been for the last three weeks upon half rations at the most and at odd times not even that ... as to clothing and boots, the battalion was in a pitiable condition."

The soldiers and others were far more critical. Canadian volunteers, dependent on the British for leadership and management of their basic needs, were greatly disappointed. A flood of personal stories and complaints from South Africa quickly passed to Canadians through letters and returning veterans. They revealed that Canadian troops were suffering for long periods of time due to inadequate food, accommodation, clothing, and medical care. During the advance on Bloemfontein, Sergeant Hart-McHarg said that despite the hard marching, they had been on reduced rations for almost a month. He recounted, "We were hungry all the time." Private Jeffery wrote, "We have been on short rations and are still mighty hungry — mighty hungry and no mistake ... have been for some time now." Private Bennett confided, "I never thought I would ever come down to eat what other people had thrown away, but after Cronjé's surrender I was thankful to eat the crumbs and crusts that I found in the Boer boxes while strolling through the deserted laager." Private Perkins wrote, "It makes our mouths water to think of a stale crust." He revealed that their general condition deteriorated constantly: "We are still weaker and there is nothing to eat." One soldier simply said, "I want to get over this hungry feeling."

Their battle with thirst was equally difficult. "Regarding water," observed Private Bennett, "many a time on the march have I and many others been glad to quench our thirst in the puddles which the recent rains had caused and some of it was as thick as mud with blue clay." Private Dunham complained, "[We] had to drink stagnant water, muddy as you could make it." One account stated, "When they reached Ramdam they hoped for water, but here they found nothing but a green slimy pool with creeping things in it. The horses turned away in disgust sniffing at it scornfully; but the men bent over and drank." The Battalion's medical officer recalled, "Men were thirsty and filled their water bottles at any source, even dirty frog ponds." Dr. A.S. McCormick wrote, "If we find water we fill our bottles by brushing away the slime from a frog pool or filling them from a pool dirty and stirred up by animals." The trek became a feat of endurance. During a four-day period the British lost 796 mules and 3,500 oxen.

Ox carts carrying supplies during the advance to Ladysmith.

Courtesy of The RCR Museum.

Equally frustrating were the uniforms that could not be replaced, but were literally in tatters. "Most of the men were in rags," explained Dr. McCormick. It was not abnormal for shoes to be missing soles, pants without knees or backsides, or shirts without sleeves and buttons. "Fighting seems to be the easiest part of the campaign," lamented Private Perkins, "no soles on our shoes, no buttons on our shirts, no knees in our trousers, no seat, it is enough to make anyone yearn for civilization." One newspaper clipping indignantly reported, "The Ragged Canadians … boots out at toes, undarned stockings bursting through gaps at the side, breeches torn and mended and torn again, here and there a pair of indigo canvas — the spoils of the enemy and the last refuge of the naked." Nights on the veldt were incredibly cold, particularly when it rained, as it often did during the campaign. Without enough clothing, a single thin blanket, and no tents, the exhausted soldiers found themselves cold, wet, and unable to properly sleep.

To try and capture the overall experience and sentiment, Dr. McCormick described:

> The rocks were hard on boots, many of which fell apart. The men were unshaven, lousy, uniforms in rags. Except when in garrison, none shaved — they were too tired at night and water was too scarce. The men were terribly thirsty and drank from frog ponds, dirty ponds — anything to get water. The order was "all water must be boiled." But after marching all day in the hot sun drinking all the water in your bottle, who would have the patience to boil the water, then wait all night until it cooled by morning.

Dr. McCormick further explained, "Some idea of how cold the nights were you may realize when I say that I put on my sweater, cardigan jacket, on the ground my rubber sheet and overcoat, then the blankets arranged in four layers and even with all this I was sometimes cold. And, of course, we slept on the hard ground." He noted that only when the Battalion served on outpost duty in Springs did they actually stay in buildings. The rest of the time the Royals were in the open air, which McCormick described as "hot days and cold nights."

But no issue drew more criticism or outrage from Canadians at home than the medical care of the sick and wounded. A Canadian officer, a medical doctor in civilian life, who visited a military hospital, was "ashamed of the professional standards." Lady Edward Cecil wrote to the British prime minister in May 1900, "Far more people have been killed by negligence in our hospitals than by Boer bullets."

Reports by journalists and soldiers soon revealed the scope of the problem. A lack of adequate accommodation, bedding and blankets, and not enough qualified, caring staff to look after the soldiers and keep them clean, sanitary, and free of flies and vermin if they were too weak do so themselves, turned a serious problem into a tragedy. And, as if things were not bad enough, men were treated according to rank rather than their illness or wound. Private Dunham recorded in his diary,

It was often difficult to determine which was the greatest enemy — the Boers or the African veldt. "Royal Canadians" on the march.

Photographer James Cooper Mason, LAC, PA-173037.

> Hundreds of men ... were lying in the worst stages
> of typhoid with only a blanket and a thin waterproof
> between their aching bodies and the hard ground,
> with no milk & hardly any medicine, without beds,
> stretchers, mattresses, without pillows, without linen
> of any kind, without a single nurse amongst them, with
> only a few ordinary privates to act as orderlies, rough
> & untrained to nursing.

The growing scandal caused one Canadian minister of Parliament to publicly announce, "Evidence is forthcoming, which goes to prove that the question of the comfort and good health, and even the lives, of our troops in South Africa has been sacrificed to consideration which we can only say call for strict investigation." The outcry in England and Canada as a result of the reports coming of South Africa about the poor treatment and support of the troops eventually led to a British Royal Commission investigation. The problems were blamed on the harsh environment and urgent needs of the campaign. Canadians felt that the British Army placed a very low priority on looking after its men, particularly colonials.

Although the harsh terrain and type of campaign were to blame for some of the problems on the veldt, others were due to the way the British Army had always been run. The fact that British regular units received their tents and replacement clothing sooner than the colonials may not have been surprising, but it made the Canadians resentful. The fact that the British Army was so incapable of providing for their basic needs added to the loss of respect for the British military and its generals. It also fuelled the growing realization that Canada would have to look after its own sons and daughters

IMPORTANT FACTS

Typhoid

Typhoid, also known as typhoid fever, is a common illness transmitted by eating food or drinking water that is contaminated with the feces of an infected person. The feces contains the bacterium *Salmonella enterica serovar Typhi*. Typhoid does not affect animals – transmission is only from human to human, and can only spread in environments where human feces or urine come into contact with food or drinking water. Care in food preparation and conscious hygiene habits, such as hand washing, are critical to preventing typhoid.

For those infected, typhoid is characterized by a slow progressive fever and excessive sweating. It can also cause a rash of rose-coloured spots. If left untreated the illness has four distinct phases, each lasting about a week. In the first phase there is a slowly rising temperature with a headache and cough. In some cases there are also nose bleeds and abdominal pain. In the second phase, the sick individual is bedridden with a temperature as high as 40 degrees Celsius. Delirium is frequent and approximately a third of the afflicted develop rose-coloured spots. In the third phase the complications set in. These include intestinal haemorrhaging, encephalitis, delirium, and abscesses. Dehydration and delirium follow. Left untreated, typhoid fever runs its course in three to four weeks. Death normally occurs in 10 to 30 percent of those infected.

With the implementation of modern sanitation practices, as well as education and vaccination programs, the impact of the disease has declined significantly.

if it wanted to ensure their well-being and fair treatment while deployed overseas. The suffering of the Royal Canadians laid the groundwork for national decisions on command and control of Canadian forces in future overseas campaigns.

For the Royal Canadians, the future consequences of their ordeal were beside the point — they still had a war to fight. A few days after their arrival to Bloemfontein, the men started coming down with enteric and typhoid fever. Within two weeks there were over 100 cases, with fresh ones appearing daily. Despite the illness, the Battalion was deployed on March 31 in reaction to Boer attacks in the local area. After a series of strenuous marches a portion of the Battalion occupied Boesman se Kop, a commanding position approximately 29 kilometres from Bloemfontein, while the remainder engaged the enemy near Waterval Drift. The next few days were spent marching back to the original camps, but the morning after they returned to the camps the Royal Canadians were deployed again. Frustratingly for the troops, the enemy was now avoiding direct engagements and the hard marching was for nothing. To add to their difficulty, it once again began to rain.

LAC, PA 185386.

Members of The RCR crossing the endless veldt.

On April 21 the 19th Brigade moved to Springfield to relieve another brigade from outpost duty. Two days later The RCR was once again on the move, in what would prove to be its second series of long arduous marches and combat that would not end until they reached Pretoria. At Israel's Poort, on April 25, the Battalion was once engaged. As the brigade's advance guard, it was ordered to seize a series of kopjes that blocked the advance. The Royal Canadians deployed in extended order, two companies up and four deep. As they approached a wire fence, approximately 600 metres from the central kopje, a "hot fire was opened upon [them]," reported Otter. The soldiers took cover where they could. Otter braved the fire and remained standing so that he could direct the disposition of the troops. As he was taking cover he was struck by a bullet on the right side of his chin, which passed through the right side of his neck. Although bleeding profusely, he remained in command for the entire engagement. After a prolonged firefight, Otter observed the Boer fire was weakening and he also heard a great deal of action on his flank. He reinforced his front rank and advanced, eventually seizing the position. The battle lasted three hours.

Although the troops disliked Otter, they respected his courage. "Colonel Otter was always very cool under fire," conceded Sergeant

IMPORTANT FACTS

Enteric Fever

Enteric fever refers to any group of illnesses in which an individual shows the symptoms of, or actually has, a fever, associated with problems related to an individual's intestines due to salmonella. The term is often used interchangeably with typhoid fever.

IMPORTANT FACTS

Pretoria

Pretoria was founded in 1855 by Marthinus Pretorius, a leader of the Voortrekkers. He named it after his father Andries Pretorius who became a national hero after his victory over the Zulus in the Battle of Blood River. The elder Pretorius also was a key figure in the negotiation of the 1852 Sand River Convention, in which the British formally recognized the independence of the Transvaal. Pretoria became the capital of the South African Republic on May 1, 1860. During the First Anglo-Boer War the city was besieged twice, first in December 1880 and then again in March 1881. The peace convention with the British was signed in Pretoria on August 3, 1881.

During the Second Anglo-Boer War, Field Marshal Roberts captured the capital city on June 5, 1900. However, a guerrilla war dragged the conflict on for almost another two years. The final peace treaty, the Peace of Vereeniging, was signed in Pretoria on May 31, 1902.

Pretoria is currently the administrative capital of South Africa.

W. Hart-McHarg, "and inspired confidence in whatever part of the field he happened to be."

Otter was evacuated for treatment and Lieutenant-Colonel Buchan assumed command. The advance continued. To the soldiers it was a repeat of the heavy marching and constant fighting. Many of the engagements were long-range small-arms and artillery fire, but the battalion experienced engagements at Eden Mountain, Thaba Bosiu, and Klipriviersberg. Otter returned on May 26 and was in command for the march into Pretoria on June 5, 1900. The 19th Brigade was the lead formation in General Sir Ian Hamilton's command, and similarly it was the battalion's turn to be vanguard within the brigade, therefore, the Royal Canadians led the occupying forces into the enemy's capital city.

The honour came at a price — only 27 officers and 411 men remained of the original contingent. Their accomplishments, however, were noteworthy. As part of the 19th Brigade, the Battalion "marched 620 miles, often on half rations, seldom on full," praised Major-General Smith Dorrien. "It has taken part in the capture of ten towns," he added, "[and] fought in ten general engagements … in one period of 30 days it fought on 21 of them, and marched 327 miles."

CHAPTER 6

A War with No End

AFTER A HARD-FOUGHT CAMPAIGN TO SEIZE PRETORIA, THE SOLDIERS were not allowed long to rest and enjoy their victory. The 19th Brigade was allowed to remain in Pretoria for only two days. Then they were deployed to secure the lines of communication. On June 11, most of the Battalion was sent to occupy Springs, a coal-mining centre approximately 30 kilometres east of Johannesburg. The British quickly established a large supply depot in the village to support operations to the north. The task was manpower intensive, due to its defensive nature and the wide area the troops needed to secure. However, the job was mostly uneventful, although some small-scale enemy action occurred. Throughout the occupation between 150 and 800 Boers remained in the area, menacing the outposts.

On June 28, 600 Boers attacked. But most of the Boers contented themselves with exchanging long-range rifle and gunfire from 1,500 to 3,000 metres away. A number of short operations and patrols were mounted against the enemy in the following weeks, but the Boers remained elusive. On August 2, 1900, the Battalion was ordered to abandon Springs, which it did the same day, and was moved by train to Wolvehoek.

The Battalion joined Major-General C.P. Ridley's mounted infantry column in pursuit of General de Wet's forces in the area of Vredefort. On August 10 the Battalion was unexplainably transferred to Major-General Fitzroy Hart's column. After many days of hard marching in pursuit of the ghost-like Boers, often without enough water, the column was ordered to return to Pretoria, which it did on August 23. "I should place on record the severity of these marches and strain to which officers and men were subjected," reported Otter, "not only were the marches long, averaging seventeen miles a day, but they were continuous; the roads very dusty; water scarce and rest most irregular."

Camp on Bloemfontein Common. Conditions were primitive to say the least.

LAC, C-3477.

FROM THE INTELLIGENCE FILES

Commando

Boers had no regular army. Instead, when something threatened the fiercely independent Boers within a district would form a militia. They would then form into military units called commandos. Each commando would elect their officers. Each member of a commando was responsible for their own clothing, weapon, and horse. Since most Boers were farmers who spent a good part of their lives riding, shooting, and surviving on the veldt they were mostly excellent marksmen and horsemen. They also understood the advantages of camouflage, firing from the prone position, and taking cover. Although they lacked military discipline they proved to be a very capable foe. During the Second World War, the British commandos who raided occupied Europe took their name from the very small, mobile, yet effective Boer military organization.

FROM THE INTELLIGENCE FILES

General de Wet

General Christiaan Rudolf de Wet was born October 7, 1854, in the Smithfield district of the Orange Free State. He served as an officer in the first Anglo-Boer War and he participated in the Boer victory at Majuba Mountain. He became a member of the *Volksraad* (or parliament) in 1897. When the Second Anglo-Boer War started he fought in the early battles as a commandant in the Natal. He later served as a general under Piet Cronje. After the British capture of Pretoria, the Boers continued the conflict using guerilla tactics. The British considered General de Wet to be the best guerilla leader. He was a key participant during the peace negotiations of 1902, fulfilling the role of acting-president of the Orange Free State. De Wet became one of the signatories of the Treaty of Vereeniging. That same year he wrote an account of his wartime experience, titled *Three Years War*. In November 1907 he was elected a member of the first parliament of the Orange River Colony. De Wet raised arms against England one more time in 1914, when he was one of the leaders of the Maritz Rebellion. However, he was defeated, captured, and imprisoned. He was released after one year after giving a signed promise that he would no longer get involved in South African politics or dissent.

The Battalion once again took outpost duty on the lines of communication. The war seemed to wind down for the Royal Canadians, and they were mostly assigned to garrison-type duties. For many of the volunteers, it was time to go home. They had done hard service — the environment was harsh, the British Army seemed incapable of, or unwilling to, properly support them, and their commanding officer seemed to lack a sense of compassion. He certainly could not relate to his men, which he soon proved once again.

On September 7, 1900, Lieutenant-Colonel Otter received a request from Lord Roberts. "I trust that as many as possible of the Royal Canadians will prolong their service until the end of the war,"

IMPORTANT FACTS

Lines of Communication

"Lines of communication" is a term still used to this day to describe both a concept and a physical reality. It refers to the need to pass instruction and orders, as well as support, including equipment, fuel, rations, munitions, medical care, mail, etc., from the forward-most troops in battle to their headquarters, right back to national command. Physically it refers to the transportation and communication network that ensures the passage of those orders, directions, and physical goods. This entails the maintenance and protection of such systems as road networks, rail lines, air transportation, and waterways, as well as telephone and satellite services.

FROM THE INTELLIGENCE FILES

3 RCR in Halifax

During the Second Anglo-Boer War the 3rd (Special Service) Battalion, The RCR, was raised to relieve the 1st Battalion, Leinster Regiment, from garrison duty at the Halifax Citadel. The war had strained the British Army manpower so much that they sought relief wherever possible. As a result, the 3rd Battalion was established – consisting of 29 officers and 975 other ranks under the command of Lieutenant-Colonel B.H. Vidal. They assumed duty at the Citadel on March 25, 1900. Although the Battalion conducted only garrison duties its service was greatly appreciated by the British government and military command. On October 1, 1902, the 3rd Battalion was officially disbanded when a British garrison resumed control of the Halifax Citadel.

cabled Roberts. After conferring with a number of officers at his headquarters, Otter responded the next day, "Your wishes will gladly be complied with." However, he had made a large assumption. All of the Royal Canadians were volunteers who had already stayed past their six-month term, and their maximum 12-month engagement was rapidly approaching. The news that they had been "volunteered" for additional service did not go over well. Obligations to family and fear of loss of employment or business in Canada caused many to resist Otter's zealous offer on their behalf. As a result, Otter was forced to recant on his offer and inform Lord Roberts that a majority of the Royal Canadians demanded their discharge in Canada, on October 15, which they were entitled to. "I deeply regret," wrote Otter to Roberts, "having misled you." In the end, 16 officers and 413 other ranks sailed from Cape Town to Halifax on October 1, 1900. The remaining 12 officers and 250 men remained in South Africa and finished out their part of the war largely on outpost duty.

On November 7, the remainder of the 2nd Battalion embarked in Cape Town on the troop transport *Hawarden Castle* for passage to England. They arrived in Southampton

IMPORTANT FACTS

LAC, C-6094.

British Field Hospital. Medical care was widely criticized for its poor standard of care.

British Shortcomings

The Boer War also prompted the British to undergo deep self-examination. The British secretary of state for war clearly spelled out the full extent of the British problems that surfaced during the war. He summarized them as:

a. Defective preparation, information and readiness for mobilization and embarkation.
b. Defective clothing for the field.
c. Defective equipment, notably in entrenching tools and in the sighting of small arms.
d. Excessive baggage and incumbrance.
e. Insufficient medical provision and transport.
f. Insufficient cavalry, mounted infantry and horses and defective equipment.
g. Insufficient artillery, both as to weight of ordnance and range.
h. Chaotic sub-divisions into divisions and brigades.
i. Unreadiness and unpreparedness of auxiliary troops.
j. Defective size and completeness of units.
k. Want of unity between the several Land Forces of the National Defence.

approximately three weeks later to a hero's welcome. They proceeded directly to London, where the next morning they marched to Windsor Castle amid the cheers of the citizens. At 1145 hours they were reviewed by Queen Victoria, who thanked them for their service in South Africa. The Battalion was then hosted for several days in England, finally departing from Liverpool on December 12 on the *Lake Champlain*. Eleven days later the last remaining members of the 2nd Special Service Battalion, The RCR, arrived in Halifax. The remaining men were immediately discharged and the Battalion disbanded.

In all, the Royal Canadians had served with distinction and demonstrated a martial spirit, endurance, and tenacity that rivalled the famous British regulars. "There are no finer troops or more gallant troops in all the world," wrote Major-General Dorrien Smith of the Royal Canadians. He was not alone in his praise. "The men of The RCR," commented the Battalion medical officer, "were a jolly lot and saw the humor in any difficulty." Even the journalists were impressed. "We have seen the First Contingent," wrote one reporter, "side by side with the bravest and the best of the imperial regiments, taking with them the hardships met with on campaign." With all of this praise, not surprisingly a Canadian veteran of the campaign revealed, "You could feel your head swelling as the truth gradually dawned on you that the term 'colonial,' instead of being the designation of a people 'a little lower than the angels' was in future to be synonymous in the military Valhalla with that of Mars himself."

Endless patrolling in pursuit of the elusive Boer commandos.

Battles of the 19th Century, 1902.

But it was not only military commanders who were impressed. The *Daily News* correspondent in South Africa was equally awed. "To Canada we take off our hats," he wrote. "She has sent us a regiment of infantry that wins admiration from every soldier for marching, endurance and fighting. It can challenge comparison with any battalion in Lord Roberts army, and that is saying a great deal."

These accolades came at a cost. In total, the Royal Canadians suffered 39 killed and 123 wounded. However, their accomplishments were impressive. After all, it was the 2nd Battalion that delivered the first major British victory in the war at Paardeberg, which became the turning point of the conflict. It also awakened a patriotism and national identity at home. The martial victory in a foreign land earned Canada, through its blood, a recognition in the international community.

The hardships endured and lessons learned became the catalyst for sweeping militia reforms that were instituted in the landmark Militia Act of 1904. Problems with command and control, supply and services, officer education and training, military autonomy, and munitions availability were all addressed. Equally important, the dispatch of distinct Canadian contingents, under Canadian commanding officers, who answered to both their British commanders and their national government, set an important precedent. The nation rejected the concept of scattering small units throughout the British field force. Instead, it insisted on a national contingent

> **IMPORTANT FACTS**
>
> **"Tommy"**
>
> Tommy Atkins, normally shortened to Tommy, is a term that was often used to describe the common soldier in the British Army in the eighteenth to twentieth centuries. The name was particularly popular during the First World War. The origin of "Tommy Atkins" is still debated. One theory is that the original Thomas Atkins was a Royal Welch Fusilier during the American Revolution. Another explains that Tommy Atkins was chosen as a generic name by the British War Office in 1815. In any case Atkins means "little son of red earth," and is in reference to the red tunic British soldiers wore during the period. Tommy (an informal version of Thomas) was a very popular English name for males. Today, within the British Army, soldiers are nicknamed Tom.

to be employed that way. From then on, Canadian soldiers fighting on behalf of the empire would do so as distinct and independent Canadian formations, responsible before all else to their sovereign government. Canada would never again blindly give her sons and daughters over to the absolute control of Britain or any other foreign power, nor would they assume that the interests of Britain were always the same as those of Canada. The Boer War had a set an important precedent — civil and military national command and control was a principle that Canada would never again forget.

Soldiers on a Kopje firing on retreating Boers during the advance on Pretoria.

LAC, C-24606.

The green volunteers seeking adventure evolved into hardened professionals who earned the respect of both friend and foe. Their blood and toil earned Canada an enviable reputation and set an exemplary standard for endurance, tenacity, and military prowess for others to emulate. They established the name Royal Canadians as one of pride and honour.

FROM THE WEAPONS LOCKER

The Ross Rifle

The Ross Rifle was a Canadian-made .303 calibre bolt-action rifle that saw service in the Canadian military from 1903 until the early part of the First World War. It came about as the result of a diplomatic argument between Canada and Britain during the Second Anglo-Boer War. England refused to sell or licence the Lee-Enfield rifle for production in Canada. As a result, Sir Charles Ross, a Scottish nobleman, soldier, inventor, and businessman quickly provided the design of his new "straight-pull" bolt action rifle as an alternative. By the summer of 1902, a government contract with very generous financial incentives and a free factory site, conveniently located in the prime minister's home riding near Quebec City, were in place. The first contract was for 12,000 Mark I Ross rifles. Although the rifle performed well on ranges in the hands of marksman, its design and construction was not well-suited to the realities of the trench warfare of the First World War. In such a dirty environment the rifle tended to jam and malfunction. Due to the many complaints and its poor performance, by July 1916 the Canadian Army replaced the Ross rifle with Lee Enfields throughout its three divisions. In total, approximately 420,000 Ross military rifles were produced. Of those, the British purchased 342,040.

EPILOGUE

THE WAR WAS NOT OVER WHEN 2 RCR LEFT SOUTH AFRICA. THE SECOND Contingent continued to fight the guerrilla war that was being waged across the veldt until May 1902, when the Boers finally surrendered. The continuing war was a savage conflict against the Boer commandos who conducted hit-and-run attacks on British outposts and their lines of communications. In return, the British and their colonial contingents manned fortified posts, patrolled endlessly, and rounded up the families of Boers and placed them in concentration camps so that the Boer commandos could not get help from the population. What British commanders had thought would be a very short war had dragged out into a very bloody three-year conflict.

In the end, a total of 8,372 Canadians (including those who served in the Halifax garrison and in the South African Constabulary) participated in the South African conflict. Of that number, 224 were killed and another 252 were wounded. Of those who died, 89 were killed in action and 135 died from disease.

FROM THE WEAPONS LOCKER

Guerrilla Warfare

Guerrilla warfare is a form of irregular warfare where one antagonist, normally the weaker, uses military tactics that depend on surprise, speed, and mobility (e.g., ambushes, raids, and sabotage) to combat a larger, better-armed and trained military force. Guerrilla forces are often composed of civilians or irregular combatants. The term *guerrilla* stems from the Spanish word *guerra*, literally meaning "little war." A guerrilla force normally organizes themselves into small, very mobile groups that can take advantage of the terrain and their speed of movement. They will normally avoid any direct combat with the larger force, choosing to strike and withdraw as quickly as possible. Guerrillas normally depend on the population to support them with food, safe lodgings, information, medical support, supplies, and recruits.

For Canadian politicians and military commanders, the Boer War experience clearly demonstrated that Canada needed control of its military forces when they were assigned to the British Army. This was absolutely necessary — not only in recognition of Canada's status as a sovereign nation, but also to ensure the well-being of its soldiers.

The war also led to dramatic advancements in the nation's military. Since becoming the minister of militia in 1896, Sir Frederick Borden had become convinced that he must improve the militia. Before the war, political patronage, inertia, and public apathy made the task very difficult. However, the conflict and the new sense of military greatness gave him the opportunity to make the changes he thought were important.

The course of the war had highlighted serious problems with supply and services, munitions availability, command and control, civil military relations, and Canada's military autonomy. Borden was committed to a broad three-point policy of producing a Canadian citizen army, distancing it from British control by making it as self-sufficient as could be afforded, and co-operative but not integrated with imperial defence.

The Boer War proved to Borden that a war effort required a modern staff system. By 1904 he revised the Militia Act — landmark legislation that established a Militia Council (modelled on the British Army Council) and allowed a Canadian to become head of the militia.

Borden pushed through his reforms and made sure that the new minister of the militia was clearly in control and that military officers, even the general officer in charge (GOC) were just advisors. As a result, episodes such as the Hutton affair at the beginning of the war, when General Hutton as the British GOC tried to manipulate the Canadian policy on whether or not to support the war, would become near impossible. The reforms also allowed for the formation of the beginnings of a modern general staff system.

The Militia Act included several other reforms. Militia strength was increased to 100,000, pay was improved, Canadian troops took over the garrisons at Halifax, Nova Scotia, and Esquilmalt, British Columbia, and an inspector general was appointed for the Cadet movement. Borden also added many modern services to the staff system. By 1905 he had consolidated 11 military districts into only five, each with its local staff and services, making command, control, and supply more efficient, especially in the case of a future mobilization. Military education was also extended. The Royal Military College of Canada was reformed and its curriculum made more relevant to modern military demands, and schools of instruction for promotion were established and passing through them by officers was enforced.

IMPORTANT FACTS

Concentration Camps

Concentration Camp normally refers to a guarded compound for the detention or imprisonment of civilians, enemy foreigners, political prisoners, members of ethnic minorities, political opponents, and in some instances prisoners of war. Conditions are typically very unpleasant. Although some scholars argue the first concentration camps stem from the 1700s, the term itself originated during Spanish military operations in Cuba from 1868–78, when the Spaniards created *reconcentrados* (reconcentration camps).

The term concentration camp came to prominence during the Second Anglo-Boer War, when the British interned Boers in an effort to curb the guerrilla war that was being waged against them. The idea was to separate the Boer Commandos from their support system. If their women and children were imprisoned, then they would be unable to provide support to their kin who were fighting. It would also pressure the Boer men to stop the conflict. A total of 45 tented camps were erected for Boer detainees. The large number of deaths that occurred in the dirty, disease-ridden camps created a scandal for the British, particularly since many of the dead were women and children. The term *concentration camp* took on an even more sinister and evil connotation at the end of the Second World War, when the Nazi death camps were discovered.

LAC, PA 185353.

The 2 RCR contingent is welcomed home on Parliament Hill, Ottawa.

The new Canadian sense of independence and militia reforms also resulted in resistance to Britain's attempts to raise an army reserve of an imperial force that would automatically involve Canada in Britain's conflicts with little to no influence or input into the decision-making process. The Canadian prime minister and his minister of militia resisted any efforts of establishing an "imperial force" for overseas commitments. In part, the moral corruption of British military leadership made Canada, as well as the other colonies, reluctant to commit military forces to British command in order to serve British policy. Canada was especially reluctant to provide Britain with military support, since support of imperial ventures had always created tension between the English, French, and immigrant populations.

Canada continued to submit annual defence plans to Britain and agreed to standardize training and organization on British models, however, overall it kept autonomy and control of its own forces. That was a hard-learned lesson of the Boer War.

The Second Contingent

Ironically, after the hard political fight for Canada to send the first contingent of soldiers, just two weeks later, on November 1, 1899, the Canadian government offered to send a second contingent, consisting of artillery and mounted infantry. The British politely declined after considering the offer for two days. The image of a unified front had already been achieved by the first Canadian contingent, so they were reluctant to take on the cost of more "ineffective colonial troops." However, the disastrous turn of events in-theatre, particularly Black Week, soon had the British government clamouring for more colonial contributions. The Canadian government dispatched the second contingent, which consisted of a brigade (three batteries) of artillery and two mounted infantry battalions, called 1 and 2 Canadian Mounted Rifles (CMR). 1 CMR was later renamed The Royal Canadian Dragoons in August 1900. 2 CMR, which was based largely on the North-West Mounted Police, was renamed 1 CMR.

Unlike the first contingent, the second contingent was actually a coalition of three smaller units that were given different tasks and that were attached to various different British formations. The second contingent numbered approximately 1,289 men. They represented the last official Canadian contribution to the war. Although other Canadians served, they were not raised as Canadian contingents. Rather, they were volunteers to formations raised by the British, such as the South African Constabulary, or privately raised units such as Lord Strathcona's Horse.

The South African Constabulary

As the war progressed the British realized that they would need an organization in the post-war period to police the defeated Boer republics. As a result, in August 1900 they created the South African Constabulary. The British government tasked Major-General Robert Baden-Powell with raising and commanding this 8,500 man paramilitary force. The Boers continued the conflict utilizing guerrilla tactics and the constabulary was used to subdue them.

Baden-Powell was both familiar and impressed with the Canadians he had seen during the war and requested as many Canadians in his force as possible. In the end, Canadians made up approximately 30 officers and 1,208 other ranks of the South African Constabulary. Many had previous service in South Africa. In many ways, the South African Constabulary was a military organization disguised as a police force. It was engaged in many campaigns and some very hard fighting. Approximately 57 Canadians died serving in its ranks.

SELECTED READINGS

Brown, Stanley McKeown. *With the Royal Canadians*. Toronto: The Publishers' Syndicate Ltd., 1900.

Churchill, Winston S. *The Boer War: London to Ladysmith via Pretoria and Ian Hamilton's March*. London: Leo Cooper, 1989.

Evans, Sanford. *The Canadian Contingents*. Toronto: The Publishers' Syndicate Ltd., 1901.

Hart-McHarg, W. *From Quebec to Pretoria With the Royal Canadian Regiment*. Toronto: William Briggs, 1902.

Horn, Bernd. *Establishing a Legacy: The History of the Royal Canadian Regiment, 1883–1954*. Toronto: Dundurn, 2008.

Horn, Bernd ed. *Show No Fear: Daring Actions in Canadian Military History*. Toronto: Dundurn, 2008.

____. *Forging a Nation: Perspectives on the Canadian Military Experience*. St. Catharines, ON: Vanwell, 2002.

Kruger, Rayne. *Good-Bye Dolly Gray: The Story of the Boer War*. London: Pan Books, 1959.

Marquis, T.G. *Canada's Sons on Kopje and Veldt: A Historical Account of the Canadian Contingents*. Toronto: The Canada's Sons Publishing Co., 1900.

Miller, Carman. *Painting the Map Red: Canada and the South African War 1899–1902*. Ottawa: The Canadian War Museum, 1993.

Morrison, E.W.B. *With the Guns in South Africa*. Hamilton, ON: Spectator Print Co., 1901.

Morton, Desmond. *A Military History of Canada*. Toronto: McClelland & Stewart, 1992.

____. *Canada at Paardeberg*. Ottawa: Balmuir Book Pub., 1986.

____. *The Canadian General Sir William Otter*. Toronto: Hakkert Publishing, 1974.

Page, Robert. *The Boer War and Canadian Imperialism*. Ottawa: Canadian Historical Association, 1987.

Pakenham, Thomas. *The Boer War*. New York: Random House, 1979.

Reid, Brian A. *Our Little Army in the Field. The Canadians in South Africa 1899–1902*. St. Catharines, ON: Vanwell, 1996.

Schull, Joseph. *Laurier: The First Canadian*. Toronto: MacMillan of Canada, 1965.

INDEX

By the Same Author

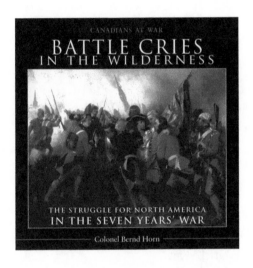

Battle Cries in the Wilderness
The Struggle for North America in the Seven Years' War
Colonel Bernd Horn
978-1554889198
$19.99

The savage struggle to take control of the North American wilderness during the epic Seven Years War (1756–63) between France and England is a gripping tale. As the two European powers battled each other for global economic, political, and military supremacy in what some have called the first world war, the brutal conflict took on a unique North American character, particularly in the role Native allies played on both sides.

Formal European tactics and military protocols were out of place in the harsh, unforgiving forests of the New World. Cavalry, mass infantry columns, and volley fire proved less effective in the heavily wooded terrain of North America than it did in Europe. What mattered in the colonial hinterland of New France and the British American colonies was an ability to navigate, travel, and survive in the uncharted wilderness. Equally important was the capacity to strike at the enemy with surprise, speed, and violence.

After all, the reward for victory was substantial — mastery of North America.

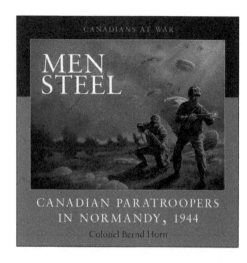

Men of Steel
Canadian Paratroopers in Normandy, 1944
Colonel Bernd Horn
978-1554887088
$19.99

Take a trip back in time to the chaos and destruction of the greatest invasion in military history, viewed through the lens of Canadian paratroopers. *Men of Steel* is the exciting story of some of Canada's toughest and most daring soldiers in the Second World War.

In the dead of night, on June 5, 1944, hundreds of elite Canadian paratroopers hurled themselves from aircraft behind enemy lines. That daring act set the stage for the eventual success of the Allied invasion fleet. From aircraft formations striking out from England on a turbulent flight across the English Channel to the tumultuous drop over Occupied Europe and deadly close combat in the Normandy countryside, *Men of Steel* is a detailed account of Canadian paratroopers and their instrumental role in D-Day.

Available at your favourite bookseller.